HANDLE WITH CARE!

HANDLE WITH CARE!

A Biblical and Reformed Guide to Sexuality for Young People

DR. JULIAN KENNEDY

Foreword by David J. Engelsma

RESOURCE *Publications* • Eugene, Oregon

HANDLE WITH CARE!
A Biblical and Reformed Guide to Sexuality for Young People

Resource Publications
An Imprint of Wipf and Stock Publishers
199 W. 8th Ave., Suite 3
Eugene, OR 97401

www.wipfandstock.com

PAPERBACK ISBN: 978-1-5326-1643-3
HARDCOVER ISBN: 978-1-4982-4021-5
EBOOK ISBN: 978-1-4982-4020-8

Manufactured in the U.S.A. 05/23/17

~

This book is dedicated to my dear wife of over thirty years, Marianna, and all the Reformed ministers from whom I have learned and gleaned over the last twenty years.

~

Contents

Part Two: The Facts of Life

Part Three: Finding the Right Mate

Foreword

A Reformed Christian, who is also a medical doctor, gives frank, clear, practical, and biblically based instruction concerning sex.

The instruction treats of the basic, physical aspects of sex, the sexual organs, and the sexual act.

The book views sex as a good aspect of God the Creator's good creation of humans as male and female. The purpose of sex, as determined by God, according to Holy Scripture, is the profound, pleasurable intimacy of marriage—the marriage of a male and a female.

From this perspective, the author warns, again frankly, against various abuses of God's good gift of sex, by both the unmarried and the married.

Among the valuable usages of the book certainly will be the use of it by Christian parents in the education of their children concerning sex and the use of it by young people to learn the truth about their body and its sexual desires and behavior.

Thoroughly practical, giving vitally important guidance regarding an aspect of life shamelessly, wickedly, and destructively exploited by the ungodly world and all too often veiled in embarrassed silence in the church, the book derives the prescribed practice of sex from the fundamental truths of the triune God, His covenant in Christ, and Christian marriage.

Scripture is characterized by frankness and openness about sex—so must the churches. May this booklet lead its readers into the joy of lifelong Christian marriage—always God's best and original plan!

Prof. David J. Engelsma

Acknowledgments

CONTRIBUTORS INCLUDE PROFESSOR DAVID J Engelsma for the Foreword and portion on singleness. Rev. Ronald Van Overloop and Rev. Ronald Hanko on dating, Professor Herman Hanko on contraception, Rev. Rodney Kleyn on pornography, and Pastor Garrett Kell on pre-marital sex. Thanks also to David Hutchings and my niece Michelle Lou Hing for their proof-reading.

Introduction

"In the beginning God created" are the first words in the Bible. Powerful words. Words that brought the universe into being at the beginning of time. Then later God said to the first human pair, "Be fruitful and multiply." Man was told to be a co-creator with God. Man was given power. Human sexuality is powerful, but like all power, it can be used for good or evil purposes. It can bless or it can curse. It's like dynamite. It can demolish a derelict building or cause innocent casualties through the wickedness of a suicide bomber. It's also akin to fire, helpful when contained but destructive when out of control!

How misled young people are today about this sublime gift of God. As Joyce Huggett says, "The ability to be fascinated by the curves and personality of the opposite sex was built-in by God way back in Genesis." And I might add, so was everything else—from the brain hormones that cause puberty and periods, to the male penile hydraulic system required to consummate the union of one man and one woman!

Sex within marriage is honorable and the marriage bed undefiled. So states God in Hebrews 13:4. Along with the rest of creation sex was declared 'good' by God. Jesus and Paul both affirmed it as part of God's abundant provision for man's well-being and also a reflection of His being and work in saving mankind in which He took a bride for His only begotten Son. It is noteworthy that Satan directed his first attack on the union of man and woman. Keep this in mind when we look at all the sexual sins and perversions.

Few parents, teachers or ministers instruct their children. The result is that young folk get perverted views from careless friends and the media.

This booklet aims to explain the truth about sex, love and marriage from the view of the Reformed* Faith of Scripture. God alone, who instituted the first marriage, can tell us what love really is and how sex in marriage can be used for the greatest benefit. Much will be said in this booklet that contradicts the popular notions about sex that are portrayed in the glossy popular magazines, newspapers and on TV soaps, in films, or in novels of today, where people hop in and out of bed and of marriages, with sad and destructive consequences to themselves and any children involved. God knows that building a lasting relationship on the rock of scriptural truth will mean it will stand in the storms of life. Prevention is better than cure, so practice godly courtship and marriage and save yourself from much heartache and many problems. The statistics on cohabitation, fornication, divorce, adultery, teenage pregnancy and homosexuality even among professing believers show how God's instructions are being ignored and it is my prayer that this booklet will help many to find God's best in love, marriage and sex.

God knows that our deepest fulfilment is the permanent relationship of one man, one woman, "forsaking all other," built on the foundations of self-giving love, trust and mutual respect. This is marriage according to the "maker's instructions."

Here is what Lord's Day 41 of the *Heidelberg Catechism* says about the seventh commandment—"thou shalt not commit adultery":

Q. 108. What doth the seventh commandment teach us?

A. That all uncleanness is accursed of God; and that therefore we must with all our hearts detest the same, and live chastely and temperately, whether in holy wedlock or in single life.

Q. 109. Doth God forbid in this commandment only adultery and such like gross sins?

A. Since both our body and soul are temples of the Holy Ghost, he commands us to preserve them pure and holy; therefore he forbids all unchaste actions, gestures, words, thoughts, desires and whatever can entice men thereto.

A Note on "Reformed"

I belong to a Reformed church and the quotation above is from a Reformed creed, the *Heidelberg Catechism*. A truly Reformed church believes in the great truths of Scripture that were rediscovered, taught and implemented during the sixteenth century reformation of the church. I believe these truths are apostolic and thoroughly Biblical and form the only sound framework for understanding God and all God's dealings with mankind. (See Appendix).

The creeds are summaries of Reformed doctrine held by many churches as their confessional standards. They can be viewed at my church website (http://www.cprf.co.uk) under "Faith."

PART ONE

What God Says

Chapter 1

Dynamite!—Handle With Care

One of the most powerful instincts we have is the sexual drive. It has the potential to bless, or bring misery if abused. It can be used for good or evil. There's nothing wrong with dynamite or sex, it just depends how it is used. If sex is accepted as a gift from God and used under His control, it will be the means of arguably man's highest earthly satisfaction. If the gift is abused, it may lead to the lowest depths of degradation. Like fire, it is a wonderful servant but a bad master. The desire for sexual fulfilment is as normal as hunger or tiredness, but God who created these inbuilt needs also tells us how to satisfy them. David Engelsma writing in the 1991 Protestant Reformed Theological Journal says "Scripture is characterized by frankness and openness about sex—so must the churches."[1]

Wrong Ideas

Sex, as created by God, was pronounced "good." Since the fall of man, his view of sex has become warped and he has become a slave of sexual desire. As soon as the first pair sinned they were aware

1. Engelsma, PRTJ 1991, p12.

of their sexuality and ashamed of their nakedness—and, of course, their sin. The world's view of sex today is that of a commodity, an animal pleasure to be satisfied as often and with whomsoever you desire, and never mind the consequences. As Christians, we have to oppose this view, believe God commands us to please Him with our bodies (I Cor 6:15–20) and offer them up to Him as a living sacrifice and continuous act of worship (Rom 12:1).

Our bodies are not the cause of sin. Jesus had a body that He kept sinless. The root of sin is in our hearts (Mark 7:21–23). Freedom from these slavish lusts comes with a new heart (Ezek 11:19). We don't have to pray that God will take away our sexual desires. He allows us to be tempted so that we can be made stronger and purer as the result of right moral choices and defeat sin. But regeneration by God through His Spirit, is vital to give us new birth and the power to overcome sin and live a holy life. Are you born again? Do you have the witness in your spirit that you are a child of God? If not, seek the Lord in His word, the Bible. Read it and listen to it preached. Find a true Reformed church or website (e.g., http://www.cprf.co.uk). Speak to a Reformed believing friend. Seek and you will find.

Chapter 2

Battle for the Mind —Impure Thoughts

"As he [or she] thinketh in his heart, so is he." (Prov 23:7).

EVERY YOUNG PERSON IS tempted by impure thoughts. Temptation isn't sin (Heb 4:15). We sin when the evil idea is allowed to stay in our minds (Jas 1:15) and when we take pleasure in it. If we reject it at once we don't sin. As Luther said, "We can't stop birds flying over our heads but we can stop them nesting in our hair!" Impurity in thought and deed (e.g., pornography) if indulged, will make us its slave (John 8:34). Job knew he had to control his eyes (Job 31:1). For men, at least, the greatest temptations come through the eyes (Matt 5:28).

Technology and Purity

In this section, which was only added recently, I want to acknowledge large portions of an article entitled "The e-world and our Teenagers" that appeared in the Standard Bearer of the Protestant

Reformed Churches on 1/1/ 2006 written by Rev. Rodney Kleyn. It is quoted below.

> "Films, TV, music videos, advertising and the internet are pervasive sources of sexual temptation to the young person. The technology that is so helpful in so many ways can become a tool that destroys children and adults, morally, spiritually, emotionally, and even physically. They, along with magazines, newspapers and billboards, parade sex as a selling tool, and "pop ups" and unsolicited pornographic sites with naked or half-naked men and women will come up on your screen at any moment on your laptop, PC or smartphone. These must be swiftly dealt with and as they are "X" rated so they must be crossed (clicked) off without a second glance—there is no other way. "Flee fornication" in this circumstance in the 21st century, becomes "flee porn! The internet can undermine parental supervision and instruction, it brings young people into unhealthy acquaintance with the ungodly, it becomes a tool for communication and rebellion between young people, it exposes them to the filth of the "sex-crazy" world, as well as exposing their identity to pedophiles and predators. These things are real. Our teenagers know it. And every parent needs to be aware of it. It used to be that parents worried about the influence of television on their children's souls. This should still be a major concern, but the concern with the internet should be greater. The computer is not just an e-mail port, but a gateway to corruption and vicious enemies of soul and life. One web site I ran across—safeonline.com—lists some facts about the Internet porn industry (back in March 2000, mind you). First, some facts about the industry are listed:
>
> 1. Over ten billion dollars is spent on porn annually.
> 2. Larger than the NFL, NBA, Major League Baseball combined.
> 3. Over two million known porn site URL's.
> 4. More than 2,500 new sites coming online every week.

5. Pornography is obscenity, not "free speech," and has never been protected by our Supreme Court.
6. Nine out of ten children aged between 8 and 16 have viewed pornography on the Internet. In most cases, the sex sites were accessed unintentionally when a child, often in the process of doing homework, used a seemingly innocent sounding word to search for information or pictures (London School of Economics, January 2002).
7. 25 million Americans visit cyber-sex sites 1–10 hours per week. Another 4.7 million in excess of 11 hours per week (MSNBC/Stanford/Duquesne Study, *Washington Times* 1/26/00).
8. Even 51% of pastors say cyber porn is a possible temptation. 37% say it is a current struggle (*Christianity Today*, Leadership Survey, December 2001).
9. 63% of men attending "Men, Romance & Integrity Seminars" admit to struggling with porn in the past year. Two-thirds are in church leadership and 10% are pastors (*Pastor's Family Bulletin*, Focus on the Family, March 2000).
10. 1 in 7 calls to Focus' Pastoral Care Line is about internet pornography (*Pastor's Family Bulletin*, Focus on the Family, March 2000).

I say it is an enemy to the soul. What is pornography, but that? It is a strong appeal to base sinful sexual desires. It destroys minds, homes, marriages, children, and more. And it is at the fingertips of those who happen to have an internet connection, at the fingertips of our children. This internet site will help us understand the addictiveness of porn: Aquila Report.[1]The first danger is the exposure of vulnerable teenagers to predators. This is a real danger. I have on my desk four different true stories of sexual predators tracking down and assaulting teenage bloggers. The most recent is the story of Taylor Behl, a seventeen-year-old who vanished from Richmond, Virginia

1. Aquila Report website.

in September of last year and whose remains were found a month later at an abandoned farmhouse. According to the Washington Post story of October 25, this teen met her killer online and exchanged messages regularly on two popular social networking sites, myspace.com and livejournal.com, prior to meeting in person. Her family was not aware of her blogging, nor her relationship with the 38 year-old, unemployed, amateur pornographic photographer with a criminal history. This is only one danger. It is less widespread, but real nonetheless. Especially when the teenagers put themselves out there as looking and desperate, using language and aliases with sexual innuendos.

The other danger is more widespread. On each blog page is a list of buddies. Each time a buddy is clicked on, it takes you to his page and his list of buddies. Soon, very soon, teenagers can be reading about and making acquaintance with other teenagers (local) who are involved in pornography, drugs, drinking parties, fornication, Sabbath desecration, cursing and bad language, movie attendance, etc. Every blogger is exposed to this. And it is all so real and so close to home, and sadly, many parents are oblivious to it. It goes something like this. A teenager sits down on a Friday afternoon to write a blog entry after a stressful day at school. Mom and Dad are not home for the evening and there is nothing to do. He notices someone has posted a comment in response to one of his blogs in which he indicated he had nothing up Friday night. It is an invitation to join them at a party promising chicks and beer. It is really that easy. And it can go in so many directions and lead to so many unhealthy relationships, web sites, parties, etc. Another danger is blogs of rebellion. Teenagers feed on each other on their sites, to stir up rebellion against teachers, parents, pastors, and others in authority. All this brings home the importance of parental guidance and supervision in the home and in the lives of their teenagers in the area of internet usage. Parents need to warn them, to lead them, to monitor them, to talk with them about these things.

I finish this article with five Internet safety tips from software4parents.com. Also worth noting are helpful websites that can monitor and exclude porn e.g., 'Covenant Eyes'.

1. Tell your child to NEVER EVER reveal their name, address, phone number or any other personal information to ANYONE online. Once you give out this information, it is impossible to retract.
2. Communicate regularly (not just once) with your child about WHAT they do online and WHO they talk to online. If you have actually met the friends they are talking to in person, you'll know it is OK for them to chat with them online.
3. Take computers out of kids' rooms and put them into public areas such as the family room. Many parents think they are helping with homework by giving the kids a computer, but it also opens certain dangers of which you may be unaware.
4. Choose your child's screen name, email address or instant message name wisely—don't reveal ages, sex, hobbies, and *certainly not* suggestive or sexy names. Predators are more likely to pursue a child with the screen name "sexyteen15" than "happygirl15."
5. Use technology to help you protect your child. Monitoring software gives you the ability to review your child's Internet usage. Even if you don't look at each and every email or instant message they send, you'll have a good idea if they are making smart choices online.

The Internet can open many doors and provide useful information for children. An aware and informed parent can help keep children safe. It is another aspect of our battle with sin and the world. May God help us in it."

Keeping pure in thought and deed is not easy, but David addressed this issue in Ps 119:11 and taking heed to God's word and hiding it in our hearts, by memorization and meditation, is the way. Taking time in devotion to God daily in reading the word and prayer is vital. Think on pure things (Phil 4:8). Your fellowship with God is worth more than the fleeting pleasure of any sin. Hear

Joseph as he remonstrates with Potiphar's wicked wife, "How then can I do this great wickedness and sin against God?" Praying when tempted to lust may help. We cannot and should not avoid the opposite sex. Monasticism, celibacy and the burka of the Muslims, are not the answer. Christ had many women disciples with whom he had a pure brother-sister relationship. Be radically pure with your eyes and thoughts! As the Lord said, if your eye causes you to sin, "pluck it out." Be radical with the sinful inclination.

Masturbation

"Character is what you are in the dark when no one but God is watching,[2]" writes Randy Alcorn of Eternal Perspective Ministries. Impure thoughts can lead to impure habits. A Christian young person cannot afford to have these. In I Cor 9:25–27 we read,

> "And every man that striveth for the mastery is temperate in all things . . . I keep under my body, and bring it into subjection: lest that by any means, when I have preached to others, I myself should be a castaway."

The same commitment that any athlete must make to train, watch his diet, and get enough rest and sleep has to be manifest in every believer to master his unruly lusts (Rom 7). This principle has bearing on a topic about which the Bible really says nothing, namely, masturbation. This is the solo act whereby a person self stimulates to orgasm (the sexual "high" or bang). Little boys, as soon as they discover their genitals, do this naturally, but it easily becomes an enslaving habit. Generally, an older boy (or girl) will indulge in sexual fantasy while masturbating and thus allow their unbridled lust to dominate their lives. Impure thoughts run counter to spiritual wisdom, power and usefulness, and self-indulgence in this way means the Spirit is grieved and we are overpowered, like Samson without his Nazarite hair. By the way incidentally, his besetting sin was lust.

2. Alcorn epm.org (end article)

This sin, and I make no bones about calling it that, because it shows an immature self-preoccupation and puts a person out of sorts with himself, is an impulse over which he has to admit he has no control, and feels guilty, and is humiliating and degrading. Of course it does no physical harm but may cause depression and certainly weakens will-power and robs a person of close fellowship with God and of usefulness in his service. It is sin because it is an abuse of God's gift of sex, something He designed to be used in marriage only. Sexual fantasy is lust in the mind and therefore breaking the seventh commandment and is the same, according to the Lord Jesus, as real adultery or fornication (Matt 5:28). By the way, the sex organs do not become useless if not used and excess sperms are released naturally at night in "wet dreams." Controlling the craving for sex through personal discipline strengthens self-control and an alert mind. If you are caught in this trap there is freedom through the grace of God. You must repent and give yourself anew to God, body and soul to glorify him (Rom 12:1). Believe He wants the best for you and will provide the perfect partner, if it is His will and in His time. John 8:32 says the truth will set us free. Sustained sitting under a good Reformed preaching ministry, personal study of Scripture, getting to know and love God, will be God's gracious means of cleansing you from this sin. Meditate on His purity and glory and desire Him above all else (Ps 73:25). Cherish fellowship with Christ. Sublimate (substitute) your desires with some regular, vigorous physical exercise, e.g., running or another sport. Seek pure friendships in the church with folk your own age, but also older and younger folk. Particularly observe godly married couples as examples. God is good. I read in scripture,

> "A wife is a good thing" (Prov 18:22).

God promises to supply all our need (Phil 4:19). Trust Him even when circumstances seem contrary as they were when Christ exhorted Martha in John 11:40,

> "Said I not unto thee that if thou wouldest believe thou shouldest see the glory of God?"

God keeps His promises, so wait in peace for the answer to your prayers. Be content with being single. God is your all-in-all. He knows what is best. If marriage is in His plan for you then you can be assured that He has the right man or woman at the right time for you, according to His good and perfect will. Trust Him (Heb 13:5; Phil 4:11, 19).

Gluttony

Overeating is related to sexual desire (e.g., orgies and the like) so be careful in your eating habits. Sexual sin abounded in Sodom along with,

> "pride, fullness of bread and abundance of idleness . . . and she cared not for the poor and needy" (Ezek 16:49).

Discipline in eating, prayer and even fasting will strengthen you. Girls: avoid "fantasy fodder" in magazines just as boys must avoid "Playboy" and other pornographic magazines. Live life in the knowledge that God is watching and is near. He cannot be mocked (Gal 6:7–8) and He always provides a way of escape when we are tempted (I Cor 10:13). If your best efforts cannot shake off sexual temptation, then call a Christian friend and seek their company. By the way, it is good to share your struggles with someone of the same sex you can trust. Confessing your faults and praying for each other is Biblical (Jas 5:16). We are in this fight together!

Wet Dreams

The spurting of seminal fluid at night when asleep is normal and should not concern any young man. It is the body's way of relieving itself of excess sperms. To sum up this section then; each young person needs to control his or her sexual passions before marriage. Victory comes through surrendering oneself to the control of Jesus Christ, recognizing that in unity with Him in His death and resurrection, sin's hold on us is broken and in presenting our bodies to Him as a living sacrifice, we are filled with His Spirit (Rom 8:2). He promises to supply all our needs just as He supplied our greatest need: forgiveness, through the cross (Rom 8:32). We should keep busy in mind and body. Satan does find evil for idle hands. Laziness leads to other sins. Switch your mind to something else whenever wicked thoughts rear their ugly head. God wants us to work hard (Col 3:23). Use your energies in physical work (or exercise), mental work, creative work and fellowship, friendship and witness.

Chapter 3

Why Wait?

THE SEXUAL UNION OF one man and one woman, what is sometimes called the consummation of marriage that normally happens on the wedding night, is something special to God. Fornication and adultery, that is, having sex outside marriage are disobedience to God and will bring His judgment and possibly other consequences such as an unwanted pregnancy or sexually transmitted diseases. Most godless young men selfishly look for the enjoyment of sex without any responsibility. This is sex without marriage, and many young women end up with babies when they were not prepared for motherhood, or they have an abortion, or end up bringing up their child alone or with their own mother's help and no father around. Friends may tease you into proving yourself, or make fun of you if you are a virgin (never had sexual intercourse). True manhood is not proven by sexual exploits, but by self-control. Joseph in Egypt in Genesis 39 is a good example of how to win over temptation and lust. His love for God was greater than the potential fleeting pleasure of sinful sex with Potiphar's wife and he fled out of the room, only to end up unjustly in jail! Fornication is the only sin we are told to flee rather than battle! Young men need to beware female enticements (Prov 5; 7:6–27; I Cor 6:18–20). Satan uses brazen, depraved, alluring women to trap men. Remember Samson. One version of these last verses says "avoid sexual looseness like the plague!" Sexual sin is sin against your own body and a believer's[1] body belongs to Christ. As a believer you are united BODY and SOUL to Christ. Your body and soul are His! II Tim 2:22 also tells us to "flee youthful lusts" and give yourself to the fellowship of the saints. Joseph when tempted in Egypt did just this literally and in the end God honored him. Adultery is sexual intercourse with a married person outside their own marriage and breaks the seventh commandment (Exod 20:14), and lusting after a woman in the mind is the same as the act of adultery according to Jesus (Matt 5:27–28). This sin is widespread among men—*ogling* would be the word! Fornication is sex before marriage and is also clearly against God's will (I Thess 4:3). God ordained the sexual union exclusively for marriage, the securest relationship into which children would be born. The sex act is the culmination of the sharing of two lives; it is when two become one flesh, and is so intimate and precious that this pleasurable total union is to be reserved for the permanent and secure committed relationship of marriage. Ignoring God's laws, which the unbelieving world will do, leads to countless broken hearts, abortions, diseases, divorces, sexual perversions and rapes. In case you think the Bible is silent on these sins you would be wrong! David committed adultery (II Sam 11) and just two chapters later his eldest son Amnon rapes his half-sister Tamar whom he then shuns in hatred, which was worse than the lust (not love!) he had for her in the first place. Sin started in the mind of this spoilt young man. This is why pornography, cheap newspapers, sex films, much advertising and even dirty jokes are dangerous—they degrade women to the level of sex objects and sex to the level of lust, rather than love, to the level of beast rather than humanity. Lust is selfish unrestrained fleshly passion that when satisfied, leads to guilt and further sin. Pedophiles and rapists and murderers started here! Lust is pure selfishness that can't wait. It is stealing what does not belong to you. But true love forgets time (and trusts God). Witness Genesis 29:20 where Jacob labors seven years for Rachel. For the Christian trusts his loving

1. Heidelberg Catechism Lord's Day 1

God (Ps 84:11; Phil 4:19). A good thing for one will be singleness, and for another, a godly wife! When physical love dominates, a relationship goes sour, conversation stops and satisfaction is harder and harder to find. This is why when courting you have to set limits on the physical side of courtship (see chapter 15 on this) and the man takes the lead in this. You are to be a spiritual blessing to your courting partner not a selfish thief taking what is not yet yours. Only a real fear of God will cause a young person to abstain from sex before marriage. If you have already failed in this area there is forgiveness to be had through true repentance. Indulging in sex before marriage is often a symptom of a desperate search for love, approval and acceptance, and really only God can give this adequately to anyone. This was one of the first consequences of sin in Eden when Adam made of Eve an idol in preference to God. After they had sinned, although Adam blamed Eve and Eve, the serpent, he made the conscious decision to be with her (potentially in hell) rather than obey God. We need to develop trusting, caring relationships and friendships with other young people. Don't spoil things for yourself or your future spouse by being pressed into premarital sex for fear of being left behind or losing your boy-friend or girl-friend. Real love will wait. Remember your friend's body will one day belong to the person they will marry (perhaps someone else), so sex before marriage will be stealing something. Sex before marriage is not only sinful but, like opening a present before your birthday, will spoil the enjoyment of it and the peace of a clear conscience.

There's a beautiful gift inside this package. It's wrapped for protection; tied for security.

Stamped *'Fragile!' 'Handle with care!'*

It's easy to loosen the strings,

To let anyone tear away the wrapping,

To give the gift without commitment—or hand out the prize for a game.

There's a gift wrapped inside this brown paper.

It's for keeps.

Non-returnable. Not to be exchanged.

It's a surprise, a happy treat to be opened by the person,

To whom it's addressed, on a date marked *'Forever'*."

By Ruth Senter. Reprinted with permission from *Campus Life Magazine*, Christianity Today Inc. (c) 1979

So, you have failed in this area and you are pregnant or got someone pregnant. What do you do? First confess your sin to God and confide in a close friend—preferably your parents—and if you are a church member, your pastor. Get godly advice, whether you should marry or not. Perhaps the baby should be adopted. Abortion is not an option, it is murder of the unborn and often leads to severe depression in the woman who has undergone it. There is support in the community and there ought also to be among family and friends. The Bible is clear that God views a newly conceived embryo as a person (Jer 1:5; Luke 1:15; Ps 139:13). So, again, I say, if you have sinned, there is forgiveness, but as Jesus said to the woman caught in adultery . . . "Go and sin no more."

Chapter 4

Homosexuality

HOMOSEXUALS ARE OFTEN GIVEN derogatory names like "queers," "homos," "poofs," "fags," etc. The biblical name is *sodomites*. They are people who are sexually attracted to others of the same sex which may or may not lead to sexual practices. David's mutual love for Jonathan surpassed the love of women, so brotherly love, among believers, can run very deep and be very satisfying. But that is not what we are talking about. This perversion of sexuality is an abomination in God's eyes (see verses below). Guilt for sin in this area needs to be confessed and the sin forsaken. Just as the alcoholic must abstain for the rest of his life from alcohol, avoid homosexual company, especially any believer who says they are homosexual. Pray much for yourself and any others caught up in this unnatural sexual trap that can and does often lead to violence, HIV/AIDS and premature death. David Engelsma writing in the *Protestant Reformed Theological Journal* in 1991 says,

> "The name of the Lord Jesus Christ and the Spirit of our God have power in every child of God who may have this unnatural desire just as they have the power in other children of God who struggle with natural sexual lusts."[1]

1. Engelsma, PRTJ 1991 p12

HIV/AIDS is a serious viral disease normally spread by homosexual or heterosexual sex but also by needle-sharing in drug addiction, as well as blood transfusion. It used to be, and in some countries still is a rapidly fatal disease, but in developed countries retroviral drugs can keep it at bay for many years. Sodomy (homosexuality) was one of the sins for which God destroyed Sodom and Gomorrah and is clearly condemned in Scripture, in both the Old and New Testaments. (Lev 18:22; Rom 1:26–27; I Tim 1:10). God made human sexuality for reproduction and Scripture teaches that homosexuality is against nature. Indeed it is a judgment from God when He gives people over to this sin. Homosexuals practice anal sex (called sodomy or buggery) and lesbians (homosexual women) usually mutually masturbate to orgasm. A Christian, if they have leanings in this sexual orientation, needs to openly seek help from an elder or pastor. There is nothing wrong with natural affection and close brotherly or sisterly fellowship with other believers, but unnatural affection or any thoughts of physical activity must be put to death. At this point I will just interject and explain why drugs are an abuse of the body. Any substance that harms your body is prohibited by God because your body is the temple of the Holy Spirit. Alcohol, in moderation does no harm but every cigarette, puff of marijuana (hash, dope), or fix of heroin is harmful and addictive. The only safe and blessed "high" or enjoyment of life is to be found in a life submitted to and in covenant friendship with Christ. He said in John 10:10, "I came that you might have life, and life more abundantly." This is eternal life, a relationship with God that surpasses any other earthly experience and lasts forever (John 17:3).

All drugs are escape from reality and have temporary effects but are inevitably followed by the crash of withdrawal. Life without God is a living death and ends in hell. No wonder people are unhappy and often commit suicide—this is because they have no hope and no human can fill their deep soul-need. It was Pascal, a famous French philosopher, who said, "In every human there is a God-shaped vacuum." Is HIV/AIDS a divine punishment? Is this worldwide epidemic due to natural consequences or divine punishment? Divine retribution in Scripture is often miraculous and catastrophic e.g., the flood, Sodom and Gomorrah, the death of Ananias and Sapphira (Acts 5) and God often sent plagues in judgment upon wicked nations like Egypt or even His own people Israel (e.g., when David numbered the people (II Samuel 24). Natural consequences are reaping what you have sown e.g., alcoholic liver disease, smoking-related lung disease etc. God's natural laws mean that our sinful abusive actions in our bodies will reap a harvest of illness. Women who force their feet into tight pointed high heels will get bunions! Individuals who prostitute themselves or indulge in homosexual perversion will reap a harvest of spiritual, psychological and physical harm and eventually eternal death if they do not repent (I Cor. 6:9). In this verse, three of the sins are sexual sins, namely, fornication, adultery and homosexuality. But the fact is, that all sin has its consequences on the one sinning and those sinned against, and God's judgment is often to give people over more and more to their sins, so that they are held fast in them and suffer for them. This is slavery to sin (John 8:34). Only God, in Christ, through His word of truth, can free people from this slavery (John 8:32 and Rom 6). The sins of Sodom, according to Ezekiel 16:49–50 were "pride, fullness of bread and abundance of idleness," no compassion for the poor, and, from the story of Lot (Gen 19), the abomination of homosexuality. Those in the church who have come out of this lifestyle need to "remember Lot's wife" (Luke 17:32) and not turn back. But Christ Himself said it would be more tolerable on judgment day for Sodom than it would be for the cities of Israel that heard His message and rejected it.

Study Questions

1. What view of sex is prevalent in the world today?
2. What do impure thoughts demonstrate? What must we avoid?
3. What is masturbation?
4. Why is it sinful?

5. What are practical ways to mortify this lust?
6. Why does God prohibit sex outside marriage?
7. What does Scripture advise regarding fornication?
8. Does the Bible relate instances of sexual sin? If so, list a few.
9. Why should we wait for marriage before we have sexual intercourse?
10. Why is homosexuality sinful? Prove it from Scripture.

Chapter 5

Two Become One

No Christian should begin to look for his or her life partner until they learn what God says about marriage. Why did God initiate this bond called marriage? Note that it is a bond, not a contract! In Genesis 2:18–25 God conducts the first wedding. In His first declaration of "not good" He saw man was incomplete on his own so He made a woman to complement him and meet his sexual, emotional and sociological needs and of course one of their main tasks as a couple was to procreate and fill the earth. The sense of loneliness he may have felt and certainly I felt, is graphically portrayed in a poem, by Michel Quoist entitled "To Love, the Prayer of a Young Man." This prayer and the imaginary response from the Lord is for, and about, I believe, the single young Christian man (or woman). See if it matches or matched some of your own feelings.

> "I want to love Lord, I need to love. All my being is desire, my heart, my body, yearns in the night towards an unknown one to love.
>
> My arms thrash about and I can seize no object for my love. I am alone and want to be two.
>
> I speak, and no-one is there to listen.
>
> I live and no-one is there to share my life.

Why so rich and no-one to enrich? Where does this love come from? Where is it going?

I want to love, Lord, I need to love. Here this evening, Lord, is all my love—unused.

Listen, son, stop and silently make a long pilgrimage to the bottom of your heart. Walk by the side of your love, so new, as one who follows a brook to find its source, and at the very end, deep within you, in the infinite mystery of your troubled soul, it is I whom you'll meet, for I call myself love, son and from the beginning I have been nothing but love, and love is in you, it is I who made you to love, to love eternally, and your love will pass through another self of yours, it is she that you seek. Set your mind at rest, she's on her way since the beginning, the way of my love. You must wait for her coming. She is approaching, you are approaching, you will recognize each other, for I have made her body for you and yours for her. I have made her heart for you, I have made yours for her, and you seek each other in the night, in my night which will become light, if you trust me. Keep yourself for her son, as she is keeping herself for you, I shall keep you for one another, and, since you hunger for love, I have in your way all your brothers to love. Believe me, it is a long apprenticeship, learning to love, and, there are not several kinds of love; love is always leaving oneself to go to towards others . . .

Lord, help me to forget myself for others, my brothers . . . and in giving myself, I may teach myself to love."[1]

Loneliness is caused by the absence of intimacy, that is, close friends. You may have lots of shallow friendships and still be lonely. To stop being lonely we must cultivate our fellowship with God. We love because he first loved us. With this as our base we reach out to love others. You only find out who you are and your place in the body of Christ when relating closely with others. True love means you care and can sympathize with the loved one and you are willing to openly share your thoughts and feelings with another,

1. Quoist, Prayers of Life, 1965.

the health and well-being of a church is directly connected with the quality of friendships within the fellowship (Eph 4:16).

Man has biological needs: food, air, water and sexual intimacy. But he has also deep social needs. Each person needs at least one other to whom he can truly open up his heart, his hurts, his hopes—marriage with a commitment to keeping secrets and loving for a lifetime provides a person with a mate to whom a man or woman can totally expose himself or herself, soul and body. We need a warm friend and an understanding companion and someone who makes up for the defects in our character. This is our God-given helpmeet. Close Christian friends of the same sex go a long way to meeting this need. Sexual intimacy is God's idea (Matt 19:4–6).

Marriage means leaving parents for the closer relationship of husband or wife. It is a covenant of mutual help, service and companionship and the sexual union is the seal of that commitment and trust. God made the first woman after seeing man's loneliness and He brought her to him. He still does this today and my marriage is an example. Adam and Eve fitted like two bits of a jigsaw. The Bible tells us that not only creation but also the whole of human history will culminate in a wedding (Rev 19:7). We, the church, will be Christ's bride. "We will see that this is the wedding all other weddings have hinted at and that this groom is the one our hearts have always longed for."[2]

2. Harris, Kissed Dating Goodbye, p168.

Chapter 6

The Proper Basis and Purpose of Marriage

Companionship and Intimacy

IN MARK 10:7–9 JESUS quotes Genesis 2:24–25 as a summary statement of the meaning of marriage. Incidentally, He clearly believed in creation and not evolution! Here He summarizes what it ought to entail:

1. Commitment or covenant—"leave and cleave," that is, the parental bond is replaced by an even deeper one which is a binding commitment. The bond is exclusive and faithful. Courting has the ultimate aim of establishing this bond. Intimacy after a public promise to love each other till death.
2. Intimacy—"one flesh"—they are one in body and soul. Flesh here is used in the same manner as in John 1:14—"The Word became flesh." They fit together for intimate ministry to each other-spiritual, emotional, and physical. They were "naked" which meant they exposed themselves unashamedly to one another. Your wife should be your "best friend." They also

should minister to others as one. God's covenant with His church/Israel is so they can know Him intimately.

3. Interdependence-head and help-meet-working together for shared goals.

It is because men and women can become so bound together; and because the breaking of these bonds does so much damage, that commitment is so necessary for healthy intimacy. This is why God's restriction of sexual intercourse to marriage is for our protection, because any other relationship lacks the commitment needed to make it safe for our hearts. Glue two pieces of paper together and then try to separate them! So that's the Biblical basis. We can go further and state that marriage is for companionship, building a home, and for sexual satisfaction. It ought to be added that for believers God ordinarily means for them to bring forth covenant children (Mal 2:14–15).

Marriage is meant to reflect Christ's love for and absolute commitment to His bride, the church, with whom He made an everlasting unconditional covenant. Incidentally this is why God hates divorce, which is separation from bed and board, but which does not dissolve the lifelong bond. It is also why remarriage is wrong—it constitutes adultery if the first spouse still lives. The only person who dissolves the marriage bond is God by the death of a spouse.

Reformed folk should attend pre-marriage classes with their pastor or elder and be prepared for guidance whether they should proceed or not. Let's look at these aspects in a bit more detail:

God saw Adam needed a helper suitable for him. In God's will, most of us need a helper. We live recognizing our need for God, but also for one another as we are social beings, but especially for that special other who will complete us. Eccles 4:9–12 states, "two are better than one; because they have a good reward for their labor. For if they fall, the one will lift up his fellow: but woe to him who is alone when he falleth; for he hath not another to help him up again; if two lie together, then they have heat: but how can one be warm alone? And if one prevail against him, two shall withstand him; and a threefold cord is not quickly broken" (i.e. the married couple and God).

Building a Home and Sexual Satisfaction

Genesis 1:28 shows us that having children was God's mandate from the beginning and it is still His will we bring forth covenant children. A godly Christian home is a powerful witness. Look at the wonderful promises in Psalm 127. The family is the building block of society.

The sexual aspect of marriage is more than just physical pleasure and satisfaction but the greatest way that two people can show unselfish love. There is nothing sinful about sex in marriage (see Song of Sol; Isa 62:5; Prov 5:18–19; I Cor 7:5; Heb 13:4).

God designed sex to be a great pleasure. Orgasm is the peak point of sexual pleasure (the bang!) when the male ejaculates or the female is maximally stimulated. Your body has the ability to be wonderfully stimulated because God made it that way. But true love involves not only sex but also tenderness, affection and genuine concern for the other's wellbeing. The friendship between man and wife is to reflect that of Christ and the church (Eph 5:22–23). Note that Christ and the church are bound eternally and earthly marriage is meant to reflect that unbreakable bond. Husbands are to exhibit a self-sacrificing love, unceasing, regardless of whether it is returned or not, a caring and protecting love, just as one looks after one's own body. Wives are commanded to submit to their husbands as the God-appointed heads of each family, confident that God is leading her husband. Any Christian girl unwilling to submit to, reverence and respect her husband probably shouldn't get married. God says marriage is for life and divorce is only permitted for proven adultery and even then it is only an option.

Separation (divorce) with a view to reconciliation should be practiced (I Cor 7:10–11). God says a believer should only marry another believer (II Cor 6:14–16). God sees marriage as a union of body and spirit. It is only to be with one person (Eccles 9:9; Ps 128:3). Marriage involves a solemn vow before God and man

(Mal 2:14; Prov 2:17; Ezek 16:8). That is why living together or "common law" marriages are not true marriages. What constitutes a marriage then? The woman at the well who had a series of lovers or perhaps husbands was now with someone who was not her husband according to Jesus (John 4). The Bible assumes a public event, civil or ecclesiastical (in church) in keeping with the country's customs, that forms the beginning of the marriage commitment.

It is surprising how much does not come out in the open during courting and engagement and newlyweds should dwell together at home to adjust to one another's faults, weaknesses and sins (Deut 24:5). Building a marriage takes effort. Faithfulness is vital and loving actions are mandated. The opposite of love is selfishness. Both of you are going to realize that it was easy living with yourself. Now you are in God's "graduate school" and you have a spouse who is not your servant, but will be your critic and will be the means of your spiritual growth. Do not be afraid to get mentoring or help from an older married couple in church. There is at the end of this booklet an appendix listing some good books on marriage and courting. Couples ought to get an early pastoral check-up from a member of their consistory to help prevent problems. Marriage ought to be the deepest and most satisfying relationship we will experience on earth. There will be none in heaven because the overwhelming, humbling and soul-satisfying, face-to-face relationship with Christ will be ours. We are told we shall be like the angels who don't marry or procreate. As Joshua Harris puts it, "Marriage is the event God has selected to consummate all of time."[1] (Rev 19:7)

1. Harris, Kissed Dating Goodbye, p168.

Chapter 7

Singleness

It is not good for the man to be alone—so said the Lord at creation. It is not good emotionally, spiritually, or physically. Singleness tends to selfishness, lack of the sanctification that having a wife and children bring and of course sexual frustration (the latter if the believer has not the gift of continence and burns). That said, God had Adam in view, when He pronounced it "not good" and he apparently did not have the gift of singleness, but others with that good gift can be happy and fulfilled in single life. As a single young woman aspiring to marriage, prepare yourself by learning to cook, sew and do other household jobs and pray for your prospective spouse. Have faith in the love, sovereignty and faithfulness of God to provide Mr. Right. Young men concentrate on your service in the church, your work or studies and your sport.

Singleness is a gift. It may be given temporarily or be lifelong. Only some are called to lifelong singleness. Our duty is to ascertain God's will and walk in it. We must be willing to accept our calling and yield our supposed rights to Him. In fact we have no rights. We belong to Him body and soul. If marriage is our calling we shall find that our spouse completes us—that is, he or she makes up for what is lacking in our own character. For the rest of this chapter on singleness I am deeply indebted to Professor

David Engelsma and his article that first appeared in the *Protestant Reformed Theological Journal* and formed part of his book entitled *Better to Marry* which follows in full:

> "Since God establishes his covenant with believers and their children, gathering his church in the generations of believers and using the godly home to rear covenant children to maturity in Christ, the Reformed emphasis upon marriage is right. But such an emphasis on marriage that ignores or even disparages single life is wrong. Justice must be done to what I Corinthians 7 teaches about the single life. After all, this too is part of biblical doctrine. Besides, failure to reckon with the biblical teaching on single life discourages the unmarried. They begin to think of themselves as second-class citizens of the kingdom. Some may even plunge into a disastrous marriage in order to escape singleness. What is even worse, if we ignore what is said about single life for some, we hinder the life of special devotion to the Lord that some may very well choose to live as single people.

Single Life is Honorable

Right in the middle of the outstanding passage on marriage, the Spirit of truth clearly and emphatically teaches that single life is honorable for some Christians. A sketch of the passage will be helpful to show this. The background of I Corinthians chapter 7's teaching on marriage is the condemnation of fornication in chapter 6:9–20. Chapter 7:1a indicates the subject and approach of the chapter which is answering questions on marriage matters. Verses 2–5 treat of the sexual aspect of marriage. Verses 10–17 prohibit divorce and remarriage. Verses 18–24 contain the important reminder to all Christians that the earthly circumstances in which they find themselves—whether racial, social, economic, or marital—become their calling from God. Believers are to accept these circumstances and live in them in the service of God. Verse 39 lays down the basic truth about marriage that governs everything that is said about marriage throughout the entire chapter—namely, the lifelong bond is only broken by death. "The wife is bound by the law as long as her husband liveth; but if her husband be dead, she is at liberty to be married to whom she will; only in the Lord."

This leaves two large sections of the chapter unaccounted for—verses 6–9 and verses 25–38. The subject in these passages is single life for Christians. The very last word of the apostle in the great chapter on marriage is praise of single life: "But she (the widow) is happier if she so abide," that is, remains single (v. 40).

Being single, being unmarried, is honorable for the Christian man and woman. Singleness as a lifelong state is honorable, (after all our Lord was single—JK). In verses 1 and 8, the apostle states that being and remaining single is good for certain Christians: "it is good for a man not to touch a woman"; "it is good for (the unmarried and widows) if they abide even as I." The word translated "good" is the Greek word *kalos*, meaning "excellent" or "honorable," especially since the thing that is good is useful for worthwhile purposes. In important respects, being single is preferable to marriage. According to verse 38, the father who marries off his daughter does well but a father who keeps his daughter in single life does better. Verse 40 teaches that, although a widow may remarry, she is happier if she remains unmarried.

The excellence of the single life is illustrated in Paul himself, and was experienced by him. Paul was single, and he found single life rewarding, indeed much preferable to marriage. The question is, in what does the goodness, or excellence, of single life for the Christian consist, and in what respect is it superior to marriage?

Devotion to the Lord

Single life is good in as much as marriage is not an absolute requirement for Christians. This is the apostle's point in verse 6: "But I speak this by permission, and not of commandment." He has just exhorted men and women in the church to marry and to live together sexually (vv. 2–5). Someone might suppose that this was a command to all without exception. Not so, says Paul in verse 6. To marry is permitted, not commanded. Therefore, single life is an option for the Christian. Singleness is an earthly way of life in which the believer may serve the Lord, as much as in marriage. Single life is preferable to marriage because it allows one to devote himself or herself more fully to the Lord and to the work of the Lord. It is not the case that single life is preferable to marriage because marriage is inherently evil, or because single life is intrinsically more spiritual and holy, or because the single Christian merits salvation by remaining single. But singleness can be useful to the kingdom of Christ. In certain instances, it is very useful. Singleness lends itself to greater devotion and service to Christ. For single life is earthly life free from the cares and troubles of marriage. Paul has a strong awareness of the problems, burdens, and responsibilities of married life. He calls these responsibilities "the present distress" in verse 26 and "troubles in the flesh" in verse 28. The everyday pressure of these responsibilities upon the souls of married Christians and the demands of these responsibilities on their time, he describes as "carefulness" in verse 32: "I would have you without carefulness." The apostle recommends singleness because he wants to spare Christians these cares (v. 28). But the purpose is not that the single Christian may be carefree, much less that he or she lead an irresponsible life. Rather, since the single life is free from the cares that invariably attend marriage, it can be devoted more fully to Christ. This is the teaching of verse 32ff. The unmarried person cares for the things of the Lord Jesus, how he may please the Lord. The married person cares for the things of the world—job, money, house, clothes, doctor bills, Christian school tuition, time for the family—how he may please wife and children. In this connection, the apostle advocates that fathers not give their virgin daughters in marriage; he wants these girls to attend upon the Lord without distraction (v. 35). The single Christian can please the Lord in a special vocation. There is place, even need, for the unmarried pastor; the unmarried missionary; the unmarried teacher in the Christian school; the unmarried full-time assistant to the deacons (cf. I Tim 5:9ff.). The single Christian can please the Lord in an ordinary vocation. The single person has more time to pray; more time to study Scripture; more time to serve the other members of the church in their needs; more time and energy to volunteer for all kinds of tasks that promote the kingdom. I say that single life can be devoted *more fully* to the Lord than married life because also Christian married life is devoted to the Lord. The apostle surely does not mean that the married believer is completely worldly, whereas the unmarried believer is completely other-worldly. Nevertheless, it is the case that the unmarried has time and energy that the married expends, and sometimes exhausts, upon the earthly cares of marriage and family.

Esteem for the Single

Important practical truths about singleness in the congregation and about the congregation's view of the singles follow from the apostle's teaching of the excellency of being unmarried. First, it is wrong for the church to suppose that everyone ought to be married and that there is something shameful or doubtful about being unmarried. The married majority of the people of God may not look down on the "old maid" and "old batch." The opening and closing verses of one of the outstanding chapters in the Bible on marriage recommend their state. Second, the unmarried themselves must not regard their singleness as failure and inferiority. Certainly, no one should plunge himself or herself into a foolish marriage, just to escape the "stigma" of being unmarried. Altogether apart from the apostle's spiritual outlook on single life, there is truth in Shakespeare's line, "Better well hanged than ill wed." Third, some single young people, as well as the widows and widowers, may well ask themselves, "Am I possibly called by God to serve him in singleness, and am I willing to do this?" There is still place in the Christian life for such devotion to Christ. There is still need in the kingdom for the work that such devotion performs.

But, fourth, the motivation must be spiritual: the single would devote himself or herself to Christ. For a young man to refuse marriage merely because he disliked the cares involved in marriage, having no intention to devote himself to Christ more fully, would not be honorable at all. The likelihood is that he will fall into the sin of fornication, or at least live the miserable life of always burning sexually.

This is I Corinthians 7's commendation, and recommendation of single life.

The One Condition

One condition qualifies everything that the apostle has to say about the advantages of single life: the man or woman must have the gift of self-control over the sexual desire—what Paul calls the ability to "contain" in verse 9. If one does not have this gift, he or she ought to marry. And since relatively few have this gift, the rule for Christians is that they marry: But if they are not able to be self-controlled sexually, let them marry! (v. 9) Even if one has this gift, he is free to marry. But if he lacks it, he ought to marry, lest he fall into fornication. This leads naturally into the teaching of I Corinthians 7 concerning holy marriage. This is, in fact, the approach of the apostle: "nevertheless, to avoid fornication, let every man have his own wife, and let every woman have her own husband" (I Cor. 7:2).

The Unwilling Single

Before we consider what the chapter teaches about marriage, a word is in order concerning a real problem with which some single Christians struggle. These are the singles who are unmarried not by choice and not because they have the special gift of being continent but because of the circumstances of their lives over which they have no control. They may desire marriage. They probably feel the need of marriage in what Paul calls "burning" in verse 9. But no one proposes marriage, if they are women, or no one accepts their proposal, if they are men. Or there are other extraordinary circumstances that make marriage impossible for them. What does Christ say to these believers? First, "let them marry" (v. 9). Do they pray about their need? Do they ask a husband or a wife from the Sovereign of the universe? Are they being too choosy about a mate, even unbiblically choosy? Is the main criterion for the man that the woman be beautiful rather than that she fear the Lord? Does the young woman turn down and turn away the young men of the church who are not handsome and dashing suitors according to the standards of the romance magazines of the world? Are both the young men and the young women waiting for the feeling of falling madly in love, when they have every right to proceed with marriage on the basis of their unity in Christ, their suitability for each other, and their warm affection for each other? It is the duty of the young men of the church to date (court—JK) and marry the daughters of the church, and it is the calling of the young women to accept the young men. This is implied in the command of verse 39, "(marry) in the Lord." Still, God makes marriage impossible for some. These Christians are to accept the single life submissively as the will of God for them. They should learn to view their single life not simply as a cross to bear but as the specific way of life in which they are to glorify God. Are they called being single? Let them not trouble themselves about these circumstances of their earthly life but serve God in these circumstances. Let them seize singleness as the opportunity to serve the Lord Christ more fully than would be possible if they were married. They may trust that God's grace will be sufficient particularly for sexual self-control. They are required to abstain from sexual relationships that is, from fornication. This is possible. Jesus taught that some make themselves eunuchs for the kingdom's sake (Matt 19:12). Not only is there the gift of sexual self-control, but there is also the powerful grace of self-discipline and chastity."[1]

1. Engelsma, Better to Marry, p35–41

Study Questions

1. What attitudes are essential to victorious living in the sexual realm? (Rom 12:1, 8:13)
2. What other two sins will likely lead to sexual impurity?
3. What industry fuels sexual sin? How do we deal with it? (Job 31:1, Phil 4:8)
4. Give three reasons for marriage.
5. What gift is essential for the single? (I Cor 7:9)
6. How should a single believer seek to meet his needs for intimacy?
7. What does the marriage bond entail
   a) at its commencement?
   b) during its duration?
   c) what alone ends it?
8. List the advantages of singleness.

PART TWO

The Facts of Life

Chapter 8

How Does Sex Start?

THE SEX GLANDS (I.E. the testes or ovaries) start to form just five weeks after conception. Both of these organs begin forming at the back of the abdomen near the kidneys—hence progeny come from their father's "loins" in Scripture. In the ovaries, cells form egg follicles and in the testes the same cells form little tubes. In later embryonic life these organs move down to the pelvis where the ovaries stay, while the testes move right out of the abdomen into the scrotum (i.e. the bag between the legs) because sperm production needs to take place at a temperature lower than core body temperature. Sometimes one or both testes don't make it into the scrotum and surgery may be required for the undescended testis. In the early human embryo you can't tell if it is going to be male or female and a very few are born intersex. The sex of the baby is decided when a sperm penetrates the egg at conception. Each germ cell has 23 controlling chromosomes (i.e. the collection of genes that you inherit) in its nucleus. The sperm has 22 plus an X or Y and the egg 22 plus an X. A new baby requires all 46 chromosomes and if the combination is 44XY it will develop into a boy or 44XX a girl. The fact that the early embryos can't be differentiated reinforces the Biblical teaching that in God's eyes they are equal in value. Neither is superior but they are different with different roles.

The man is to lead, initiate and make decisions, and the woman to help, add her sensitivity and follow. (Gal 3:28). This means that despising or repressing women as happens in some cultures and notably in the religion of Islam is wrong.

Chapter 9

Men versus Women—What's the Difference?

Men

THE SEX GLANDS, TESTES or testicles, the primary sex organs are oval-shaped organs—little factories that make sperms and a hormone called testosterone that produces the secondary sex characteristics (the manly traits), i.e., beard, body hair and muscles. Sperms—tiny microscopic tadpoles—are made from puberty onwards until old age in the testes in the scrotum, which when the body is warm will hang limp but when it's cold will retract to keep the testes at the right temperature. The epididymis is a coiled tube behind the testis where sperms grow and are stored. The vas deferens is the long hard tube which is muscular and contractile leading from the epididymis to the urethra that carries sperms. The urethra is the tube leading from the bladder that carries urine and also sperms during intercourse at ejaculation. The prostate gland, just below the bladder, makes fluid to feed the sperms. Semen or seminal fluid consists of sperms mixed in the secretions of prostate and seminal vesicles which is ejaculated during intercourse. The penis is a spongy organ which can fill with blood and by ingenious hydraulics involving valves, become erect and hard, capable of insertion into the female vagina during intercourse. The act of intercourse causes myriads of nerve impulses to go to the brain and spinal cord which eventually lead to the explosion of sperms from the vas deferens and the peak of pleasure called orgasm.

Women

The labia majora are large soft lips of thick skin and fat covered by hair that protect the labia minora which are small thin moist lips that partially cover the vagina. The clitoris is like a small penis with no opening, very sensitive, lying at the uppermost end of the labia. When stimulated it contributes to female orgasm or climax. The vagina is the passage between the outside world and the womb (uterus). A female virgin (someone who has never had sexual intercourse) has a partial membrane over the entrance of the vagina, called the hymen, which when first torn leads to minor bleeding (the tokens of virginity, the bloodstained sheet in the Old Testament). The vagina receives the erect male penis during sexual intercourse and is kept wet by glands. It has the ability to stretch enormously to allow the birth of a baby. Down the vagina each month flows the blood of a period (menstruation), which is "the tears of a disappointed uterus." The lining of the womb, which has built up over the first fortnight of the cycle, is shed along with some blood if the egg, released around day 14, is not fertilized. This happens on several days, e.g., days 1–5 when a new cycle begins. The ovaries are small round organs on the sides of the pelvis which each month take turns to produce an egg which is released, finds its way into the fallopian tube and may or may not be fertilized on its way to the womb, by sperms coming up. The ovaries also secrete the female hormones that lead to women's secondary sex characteristics, i.e., breasts, thin waist, wide hips and body fat. The uterus is a pear-shaped organ inside the pelvis in which a conceived baby grows protected till birth. The bottom end opens into the vagina and is called the cervix and is more fibrous than the muscular womb. Contractions of the muscle of the massively pregnant womb lead to gradual opening of the cervix and the expulsion of the baby at birth.

Conception

During sexual intercourse in which the man's penis moves up and down inside the woman's vagina, excitement reaches a climax at male ejaculation and millions of sperms are released into the vagina and are sucked up into the womb and by muscular contractions moved upwards through the womb and along the Fallopian tubes where they may nor may not meet the egg.

If they do meet up, the sperm tip has an enzyme that enables it to penetrate the egg's coating and discharge its nucleus into the egg to fertilize it. The egg then is milked along the tube into the womb where again powerful enzymes on its membrane allow it to burrow into the thick womb lining to implant itself. All these "irreducible complexities" show any evolutionary theory to be bunk! The female menstrual cycle is designed to prepare the womb for a fertilized egg. The egg grows in a follicle for two weeks, while the womb lining thickens. Then it is released and possibly fertilized mid-cycle. If the egg is not fertilized, it dies and along with the womb lining it will be shed at the end of the month during the menstrual period. The egg, no larger than a full stop (in the US a 'period'), only lives 12–24 hours. The sperms, 2,500 of which could cover a full stop, can live 24–48 hours and once the egg is penetrated an ingenious system prevents further sperm penetration. The hormones that are produced by the broken egg follicle (progestagens) prevent the womb contracting and stop other eggs forming—so there are no more periods during pregnancy. Twins are formed in different ways. Non-identical twins form when two eggs are simultaneously fertilized. Identical twins form when one fertilized egg splits into two parts, each of which forms a new baby. The process of conception to birth is a miracle. Answers in Genesis organization has wonderful DVDs to illustrate this (check out their website).

Chapter 10

Boy Meets Girl

There is something in all of us that makes us want the company, friendship, and admiration of the opposite sex. Normally our ideas about the opposite sex change around puberty (i.e. the age a boy becomes a man and a girl becomes a woman). This usually occurs, in boys, between the ages of 14 and 16, but can be as early as 12 and as late as 18. Girls enter puberty usually at age 12 to 14 but this can range from 10 to 18. Before this age boys usually prefer the company of boys and girls likewise, but with puberty an attraction for the opposite sex develops. This process, adolescence, is making a unique adult, different from everyone else, and attracted to the opposite sex. Young children's attitude to sex can range from complete apathy to acute consciousness that may lead to lots of questions and possibly experimentation. For the last century girls have been starting their periods (called menarche) at an earlier age. In 1844 it averaged over 15 years and in 1984 it was 13. In some poor countries it is not unusual for girls to have their menarche (first period) at 9 or 10 years. It is important that girls are prepared for this and that boys also be prepared for wet dreams which is the unconscious emission of sperm during sleep. Parents need to have the facts and be ready to teach their children. What happens at puberty? Girls notice their breasts enlarging, pubic hair growing and the figure developing with widening hips and a narrow waist. The ovaries start releasing an egg monthly and periods (menstruation) start. Some internal clock in the brain (pituitary gland) begins this process. Hormones from the pituitary make the testes and ovaries wake up and start making their own hormones. As these physical changes happen, both boys and girls begin to be really concerned about how they look. They begin to choose their clothes, may appear moody, selfish and very emotional, and though they want to befriend the opposite sex they may feel very shy.

In boys, later than girls, the pituitary switches on the testes which grow, begins to release testosterone and then the penis grows, hair begins to grow on the face, body and pubis, muscles enlarge and the voice box (larynx) also enlarges and the voice breaks (deepens). Some boys pass through a stage where they are attracted to their own sex. This normally is temporary and soon passes but it is vital that homosexual thoughts, sinful as they are, are never allowed to become homosexual behavior. Does it matter if you have a boyfriend or girlfriend? No. Many don't have friends like this till much later. The important thing is to have friends of both sexes, especially Christian friends. Getting too serious too early can be tragic and many will testify to ruining their lives by getting intimate and/or marrying very young. The young Christian male is to treat his believing sisters with all purity just like his own sibling sister (I Tim. 5:2). Avoid giving any Christian girl the impression you are interested in her till you have gotten good advice from someone who knows you both. When should you marry? Maturity comes at different ages but a rough guide of 20 for girls and 25 for men is reasonable. The truth is, when God brings two people together and they are mature enough, and by their courting become convinced God has brought them together and that godly advice and teaching by elders and mature believing friends who know them both, agrees, then they are ready to marry.

Chapter 11

Friendships

"Life without friendship is like the sky without the sun"—so says a fridge magnet we were given. Friendship is what makes life worth living—primarily, friendship with God through Christ, who is not ashamed to call us brothers and sisters, but also friendship with His people. Loneliness can be very depressing and you can be lonely among a big crowd or even so-called "friends" as I was at university. Do you know why that is? Remember the prodigal son? No-one cared for him at all. Before I was converted, like all my friends, I was selfish, so all I cared about was me. Not even my close family could meet my deep need of salvation and forgiveness. The first Christians I met genuinely cared for me, inviting me to their homes etc. You may have lots of non-Christian friends and be very empty and lonely but real love comes through friendship with God and His people. To enjoy this, sin has to be dealt with at the cross of Christ. There is no doubt that mutually enjoyable activities like sports and other hobbies can lead to worldly friendships of the "*phileo*" variety but what we yearn for and need is "*agape*"—unselfish love—love that gives as Christ gave Himself. The only love that satisfies a human being is the unchangeable, unconditional love of God in Christ. And when we know and experience it, we can give it out (I John 4:7). Among believers intimacy is fostered by fellowship, which means caring, sharing, working, worshipping, praying and playing together. At the heart of fellowship is communicating and listening, showing genuine interest and interest that leads to prayer for the person. It's best to stick to same-sex friendships like David and Jonathan, while you are single, but obviously you need to be in the company of the opposite sex when you are getting to marriageable age. So as a young single person pursue friendships especially with folk of the same sex in church.

Life without friendship is like the sky without the sun. What does Jesus' life teach about friendship? His best friends were the disciples (John 15:15) with whom He shared intimately and openly. How did He do this? By,

1. Spending much time with them.
2. Telling them about Himself and His purpose.
3. Telling them about themselves.
4. Caring for them by acts of loving service, e.g., washing their feet.
5. Working with them in proclaiming the gospel.
6. Ultimately dying for them. "Greater love hath no man than this, that a man lay down his life for his friends" (John 15:13).

The covenant relation between the Trinity (tri-unity) of God—Father, Son and Holy Spirit—is the infinitely deep and absolutely perfect relationship of family friendship and forms the basis of all derived friendships particularly that where His people are taken into His friendship by grace. The friendship between the Father and the Son is one of mutual honor, delight, love, respect, trust and certainty. The Holy Spirit is the personal bond of love that binds them, just as He binds Christians to Christ and to one another. We could list the ingredients of a satisfying friendship:

1. Understanding each other's desires and aims and being united with them.
2. Freedom in sharing and giving.

3. Desiring what's best for the other.
4. Enjoyment in the company of the other and openness to include others.
5. Loyalty and trust.
6. Respect and mutual submission.
7. Sustained closeness even in separation.
8. Forgiving and forgetting.
9. Praying for each other.
10. A hug, kiss, or handshake as appropriate.

It goes without saying that we are to love all our brethren in Christ whether we like them or not. What about unbelievers? Relationships with them as a basis to share Christ should be the aim. Our lives are a powerful witness (John 16:15). But we need to watch that they are not negatively influencing us (Ps 1).

With whom do you live when you leave home? Try to share accommodation with believing friends and never in a mixed-sex flat because that is a bad witness and a ridiculous temptation (I Thess 5:23). Even with believing friends there will be issues as your different habits and inherent selfishness will lead to misunderstandings and rows, but this can lead to spiritual growth. Don't keep yourself to yourself as I once did, and hence felt very lonely and left out. Share with and serve the others!

The journey from friendship to engagement is covered well in *Boy Meets Girl*, by Joshua Harris[1] and I have summarized it later.

1. Harris, Boy meets Girl, p73–86 and 196–209.

PART THREE

Finding the Right Mate

Chapter 12

The Meaning of Love

"Crush" or True Love?

How can I know if I've got a "crush" which is generally emotional and selfish, or true love?

A "crush" is:

1. Often sudden.
2. Based on physical beauty or charm.
3. Not based on knowledge.
4. Idealizes the person.
5. Not open to advice.
6. Self-centered.
7. Haste to mate.
8. Insecure.
9. Artificial behavior.
10. Feels it must act.

Contrariwise, true love is:

1. Something that grows.
2. Based on character or spiritual qualities.
3. Based on friendship.
4. Realistic.
5. Open to advice.
6. Real concern for the other person.
7. Patient for marriage.
8. Secure.
9. Trusts God and waits.

A "crush" or infatuation can develop into true love but check what kind yours is and wait God's time. True love can wait and trust God's goodness and timing. His work is perfect and all His ways are just. The thrill caused by closeness to a member of the opposite sex is often mistaken for true love and a marriage based on a "crush" doesn't usually last. Listen to Harris, "For the person practicing the self-centered, feelings-governed, beyond my control love of the world, God's definition can be as startling as an unexpected slap in the face. Christ taught (and exemplified—JK) that love is not for the fulfilment of self but for the glory of God and the good of others."

In the Greek there are three words for 'love.' They are *agape, philia* and *eros. Eros* refers to sexual attraction and sexual love, the union of two bodies. *Philia* means the affection and love of friendship where normally there would be similarity of interest, e.g., sport. *Agape* is Christ-like love. It is the unconditional and eternal love of God towards His people. It is the love expressed in the cross and felt in us by the Spirit, who is given to us (Rom 5:5), and that we can express too because we are empowered by the Spirit and exhibit His fruit (Gal 5:22–23). It is a self-giving love that serves; not an emotion, but an act of the will that does not depend on the likeableness of the other. It loves enemies and unattractive people. It is exemplified in marriage vows where lifelong faithfulness is pledged to the other in whom there is delight and spiritual unity.

Thank God that He does not fall in and out of love with His people! God's true love clashes with dating as we know it. Harris states: "It seems that dating as we have come to know it doesn't really prepare us for marriage; instead it can be a training ground for divorce. If dating causes us to practice selfish, feelings-governed love that's contrary to God's love, we must be willing to reject it."

In the courtship and subsequent marriage of a believer all these loves should exist with the *spiritual* attraction being basic, *philia* next, and, after marriage, *eros* (in its full expression) in the consummation, usually on the honeymoon—i.e. during first sexual intercourse. The Holy Spirit alone leads you to the person God has chosen to be your life-partner and ideally they should be the first and only one you fall in love with. God brought Eve to Adam. How careful we need to be! Emotions must not be allowed to lead us because they often deceive us. Selfish "love" (which is actually lust) is manipulative. Feelings should follow the will to love. This only happens when we crucify our own desires and seek God's will. Whenever we are attracted to someone we should try and keep it under the Spirit's control. Pray much for God to reveal His will and get advice from others. God is never late and never makes a mistake. Proverbs 4:23 says "Guard your heart" (i.e. your affections). This is because they influence everything else. God knows the *exact and ideal person* for you and can be trusted to bring you together, if it is His will that you marry. After all, He has been the divine matchmaker since time began. Someone has rightly said that it is a selfish act to show special affection to someone you don't intend to marry. As and when the relationship develops you must discuss, among other things, having and rearing children, home and finances, in-laws, and, if possible, attend marriage classes at your church. Here are some very important questions that will guide you.

Is your prospective friend a believer, specifically a *Reformed* believer? (Amos 3:3).

Is your purpose in life to glorify God whatever the cost? (Ps. 34:4). How does he/she use his/her time?

1.Do you share some common interests?

2. Do you honor and respect and trust each other?
3. Can he/she provide for you and be father/mother to your children?
4. How does he/she handle money?
5. Do you share openly with him/her? (John 15:15).
6. How does he or she take care of his or her body?
7. Are you willing to give her/him your soul and body for the rest of your life?
8. Do you get on with future in-laws?

As you contemplate whether the courtship is heading toward marriage here are Joshua Harris' questions:

1. Is your relationship centered on God and His glory?
2. Are you growing in friendship, communication, fellowship and romance?
3. Are you clear on your biblical roles as man and woman?
4. Are other people supportive of your relationship?
5. Is sexual desire playing too big (or too small) a part in your decision?
6. Do you have a track record of solving problems biblically?
7. Are you heading in the same direction in life?
8. Have you taken into account cultural differences?
9. Do either of you have complicating entanglements from past relationships?
10. Do you want to marry this person?
11. Do you perhaps realize this relationship should not progress to the altar? Then kindly break it off and save yourself lifelong regret and sadness.

Chapter 13

Finding Your Help Meet

GOD ALONE CAN LEAD you to the person best suited to be your life partner. He is committed to His plan for each of His children (Jer 29:11). It is one of the most important decisions of your life. I prayed and waited for 12 years. God makes promises in Psalm 37:4, Matthew 6:33, 7:11 and Ephesians 3:20. Differences in culture, color, or even parental objections (particularly if your parents are not believers) must be seriously considered, but they, and other potential problems, are nothing to Almighty God. If your parents are Reformed believers they have a covenantal obligation to supervise carefully the courting of their young people and the young people (their offspring) should be thankful of this concern and not consider it intrusive. So listen to your parents. To do otherwise is to court disaster as happened in Ezra's day (Ezra 9:2–3, 12; see also Mal 2:11). There ought to be unity of spirit between potential spouses and among Reformed believers. That means mutual membership in a Reformed church. Hear what Rev. Angus Stewart of the CPRC in Ballymena wrote in a recent website article:

> "Turning to something even more obviously practical and immensely personal for young adults, the creeds (and the Reformed faith they summarize) help in courtship and marriage. If Scripture requires of church members

> that "all speak the same things," being "perfectly joined together in the same mind and in the same judgment" so that there are "no divisions" (I Cor 1:10), how much more ought this be the case with that person with whom you are contemplating becoming "one flesh," that is, "one body" and "one spirit" (I Cor 6:16–17)? Can two walk together except they be agreed? (Amos 3:3). How then can a man and a woman walk together in marriage (usually for decades) until death them do part, except they be agreed? This involves living together; eating, drinking and sleeping together; praying and worshipping together; engaging in church life together; training children together; working their way through hardships together; confessing their sins against each other; etc. Thus young Reformed adults must date and marry only those with whom they are doctrinally united—united in the creeds. Both must be able to confess the same truth with "I believe," before they can say, "I do."[1]

No-one is obliged to obey parents or submit to arranged marriages if the proposed partner is an unbeliever. Proverbs 19:14 says that a prudent wife is from the Lord. Look for the fruit of the Spirit—someone who is zealous for the Lord. The girl should possess "a quiet and gentle spirit" as per I Peter 3:4, and the wife of Proverbs 31:10–31 is characterized by "the fear of the Lord."

In the Lord's eyes, a girl is only as beautiful as she is holy. She should be someone who will pray, read the Bible, sing with you, not be someone who is bossy, noisy, too talkative or too concerned with outward beauty. Do you share other interests? Does she help you spiritually? Is she open and honest? Are we physically attracted? Are our ages compatible? There are many beautiful mixed-race marriages of which mine is an example. If, after weighing up everything you are not sure, wait! Our Good Shepherd promises to lead (Ps 32:8). Finally, steer clear of any proposals or emotional entanglements till some months after any disappointments or break-ups or a death in the family and never marry out of sympathy.

1. Stewart, Importance of Creeds for Christian Youth, on-line.

Chapter 14

For Girls Only

Women are made differently from men—that's obvious! Physically, mentally and emotionally different. Because a woman is made to be a mother, she is more sensitive, more subjective and more emotional than a man. In women we see the motherly qualities mentioned in Isaiah 66:13 and Matthew 23:37. The great glory of a woman is the gentle and quiet spirit of I Peter 3, and tenderness, not necessarily outward beauty. Women have sexual instincts but they are more passive and easily controlled. A woman longs for attention and love, to have a home and family. Women naturally attract men, but for the Christian girl there must be modesty in dress.

The Scripture in I Peter 3:3–6 is addressed to wives but equally applicable to all women. They need that deep inner beauty seen in the saintly women of old who trusted God and submitted to their husbands. The God-given power to attract the opposite sex is generally badly abused in the world. We see whorish make-up, half-naked bodies, elaborate and weird hairdos, tattoos and piercings. We see from I Timothy 2:9–10 and Isaiah 3:16–24 that our bodies and dress are to glorify God. It is important as Christ's sisters to dress neatly, attractively and simply, and never to provoke lust. Remember: true beauty is *internal* (Prov 11:22).

In Genesis 3:16 we read, "and thy desire shall be to thy husband, and he shall rule over thee." The desire will be *to rule* (Gen 4:7). Under God's curse, the woman desires not only to have the man but to *control* him. This will be the characteristic of women who are obsessed with beauty and with captivating men. Eve wanted to usurp Adam's place under God—her desire serves her own ends rather than God's glory and the well-being of the man. Her desire weakens him rather than helps him. Because of the curse, feminine sin involves disrespect toward men, challenging for control, belittling comments, incessant nagging and exploiting his weaknesses, all in the place of godly respect, and for the rule that God gave him in the relationship. This is what lies behind feminism and women in church office. As a believing woman see that you are not guilty of this role reversal. What to look for in a prospective husband? A girl needs a godly man who will spiritually lead her, protect her and give her a sense of security; one who cares for her, helps her, comforts her, understands her and inspires confidence in her—someone on whom she can truly depend (like Christ). Love grows out of respect and admiration which are vital.

> "A man shall be as an hiding place from the wind, and a covert from the tempest; as rivers of water in a dry place, as the shadow of a great rock in a weary land" (Isa 32:2).

Chapter 15

Courtship, Dating and Right Relationships

This chapter has had a significant revision since I first wrote it! I even had to ditch the old title "Dating" because I think that the term has too many worldly overtones, for we are called to be *in*, but not *of*, the world. "Courtship" is a better word. However the problem is not in the term but rather in our sinful natures, although it has to be said that dating grew out of a culture celebrating self-centeredness and immorality. Joshua Harris, in his book *I Kissed Dating Goodbye*, realized he had messed up too many lives, including his own, playing the "dating game" and made a radical decision to give it up and "make pleasing his Lord the priority." His attitude changed from getting his own way, to loving *Christ's* way and seeking the other's best interests, wanting their purity and holiness because that pleased God and served to protect him and her. This brought him great peace and joy. Check out the definition of biblical love:

> "Charity suffereth long (is patient), and is kind; charity envieth not; charity vaunteth not itself, is not puffed up, doth not behave itself unseemly, seeketh not her own,

> is not easily provoked, thinketh no evil; rejoiceth not in iniquity, but rejoiceth in the truth; beareth all things, believeth all things, hopeth all things, endureth all things. Charity never faileth" (I Cor 13:4–8).

Harris states clearly that love is not to fulfil self, love is not a feeling, and love is not beyond our control. And Paul's admonition in I Timothy 5:2 was to treat "the elder women as mothers; the younger as sisters, with all purity."

Rev. Van Overloop of the PRCA (Protestant Reformed Churches in America), who has written a booklet on this, is extensively quoted shortly. Meantime let me pass on his definitions, I have replaced "dating" with "courtship."

> "[Courtship] is the middle stage in the process of finding a suitable mate. The first stage is mixing with potential mates in a good Reformed church. The final stage is engagement and marriage. [Courtship] comes between friendship and getting engaged. [Courtship] leads to marriage. Because of this you may not [court] just anyone, no-one who may not become a lifelong mate."[1]

Harris, in relation to courting/dating says that a man has no business asking for a girl's heart and exclusive affections if he is not considering marriage. If you are not ready for marriage, wait for romance. Harris and his girlfriend, Shannon, had agreed that their relationship was very clearly with the purpose of finding out if God would have them marry, and in his own words: "see the good, the bad and the ugly in the one we love." Short term romance and the desire to enjoy emotional and physical intimacy without the responsibility of real commitment are sinful. In other words, courting should be exclusively for those ready for marriage. Courting is taking time to be with someone of the opposite sex in order to get to know them, with the main purpose of developing a oneness of spirit and deep friendship which when pursued should be the basis for engagement and marriage. It should not be

1. Van Overloop, Sex and Dating, p3

entered into lightly. Perhaps in church it is best if relationships are confirmed by the parents and the pastor.

Courtship may be a group activity or just a twosome. It can be a walk in the park, playing a sport or a meal in a restaurant. Some Christians take the first date very seriously and would not embark upon it without much prayer and counsel and some assurance that God is leading in the relationship. I agree this is wise. Courtship should not cut a couple off from others, indeed it should be pursued in the presence of others. The couple need to see each other in the real-life settings of family and friends. Others believe it is not such a big step and that young people should date a few people to ascertain God's choice. I believe the first option is scriptural as in the Bible many examples show us that waiting is often part of His plan and that He can be trusted to organize the meeting of the two who are destined to become one and we don't need to "play the field" e.g., Moses and Zipporah, Isaac and Rebekah, Boaz and Ruth. Adam and Eve, our classic, most ancient parental pairs are good examples. Even Adam himself did nothing (except sleep) and God brought his wife to him! But that does not mean we are to be completely passive. Here is a quote from "Courtship, Dating and Right Relationships," by Tracey Bartolomei:

> "For those who are disappointed with the results of the dating scene, an alternative is now gaining popularity. Before automobiles and the information age, those eligible for marriage practiced a custom known as courtship. Some grandparents can probably still remember the days when young ladies did not go out with men unchaperoned. Instead, family and group activities were the most common and accepted form of socialization between the sexes. When a couple believed that their interests could involve ones of eventual marriage, they began some form of courtship. Courting was used to becoming better acquainted with the other party and his/her family. Family involvement generally played a significant role in the courtship process. The practice of courting has been a vital part of the Judeo-Christian culture for thousands

> of years. This old-fashioned idea is currently gaining a following of singles that are looking for smarter ways of tying the knot and keeping it tied."[2]

With the AIDS epidemic and a divorce rate hovering over 50%, many are expressing strong concerns in the area of relationships and marriage. Most marriage counsellors now recommend taking a more "preventive" approach to marriage. It is much easier to have a healthy lasting marriage if you don't enter with a lot of "emotional baggage" from past relationships. Counsellors say that the key elements to a successful marriage are friendship, compatibility and strong communication skills. Courtship is viewed as a viable means of developing these elements. The main difference between dating and courtship is the attitude that one assumes towards relationships and the activities in which the couple engages before marriage. Contemporary dating is generally a self-focused pastime. Courtship doesn't actually begin until each feels that the other person could be a prospective marriage partner. Their time together is spent getting to know each other better through conversation and group socialization, rather than sexual intimacy characterized by expectations of physical or emotional intimacy without commitment. In dating, self-gratification is paramount. If either party is no longer gratified, the relationship ends—thus, a cycle of short-term relationships begin and continue. In courtship, both individuals have the understanding that marriage is the eventual goal of the relationship. Courtship takes a more thoughtful, long-term approach to a premarital relationship. The emphasis is on developing friendships and seeking. Various Christian books and recent radio programs have given much attention to the subject of courtship. Josh Harris' book, *Why I Kissed Dating Goodbye*, and Elizabeth Elliot's *Passion and Purity* are two top sellers. The Internet is another excellent resource. When courting, start with prayer. In *all* thy ways acknowledge Him (Prov 3:5–6). It should be natural to bring your Lord into every aspect of life. Fellowship between believers and particularly between a courting couple should

2. Bartolomei, Courtship, Dating and Right Relationships, on-line.

involve the reality of Christ and His work in us and what He is teaching us. Harris has this to say about listening,

> "Communication is more than speaking; it is listening; understanding and properly responding to what we have heard and listening is an expression of humility and genuine concern for others." [3]

Courtship should aim to assess each other's character, attitudes, values, opinions and convictions about life. In a section at the end of his book on courtship, Harris enlists the help of his two editors to suggest ideas for "courtship conversations." Here are some and they can just as easily involve others:

- The story of me—share your baby photograph book and other photos and memories (family, school, Christian life).
- Cook a meal for each other.
- Play board games like Scrabble or Boggle and/or discuss sporting interests.
- Do a craft or service project together e.g., helping someone decorate.
- Babysit for a large family.
- Decide where the best budget dinner for two can be got and discuss money management.
- Go on a lunch or dinner with a longtime married couple.

As your confidence for future marriage increases you will want to discuss topics relevant to marriage. Be careful to set behavior standards from the outset, regarding physical contact. Petting, which is any intimate physical contact, once started, is impossible to control and is sinful. It is really the prelude to intercourse and should be confined to marriage. Remember the analogy of fire or the fuse: useful while under control, but dangerous when out of hand. There's nothing wrong with holding hands and a short kiss, but passion must be kept under control. Some have argued that

3. Harris, Boy meets Girl, p94.

even the first kiss should wait till the altar—now that is a high but commendable standard! Harris stated in his first book his commitment to waiting even for a kiss until his wedding day. He quotes with real insight what Solomon says in Ecclesiastes that there is a time to embrace and a time to refrain from embracing. Harris and his girlfriend set out specific and detailed courting standards or "fences" or "yellow lines" they would not cross which can be read in his book, *Boy Meets Girl*, under the heading "Our Guidelines"[4]—they make interesting reading! He also refrained from saying "I love you" till he proposed marriage and real commitment was his aim. Make sure you are up-front and honest about past relationships which were either innocent or sinful.

Here are some guidelines:

1) As far as friends, relatives and unbelievers are concerned, abstain from every appearance of evil (I Thess 5:23). Never be alone in a car, someone's home or elsewhere, late at night.
2) Flee youthful lusts.
3) Keep your conscience clear.
4) Treat your girlfriend or fiancée as your sister (which she is in the Lord) on your date. You should be able to share everything with her.

Remember Christ the Lord is part and parcel of your attraction. It is best to not turn on the ignition of the sexual motor car until it is time to drive off when you are married! Listen to the advice of Rev. Ronald Hanko[5]:

"Be very careful that your love for one another does not draw you into sin. Courting couples must be careful about the hours they keep. They must be careful about how often they see each other.

They must be careful how they spend their time together. Not spending a lot of time alone together, unless perhaps on the

4. Harris, Boy Meets Girl, p83.
5. Study Outline Queens Univ. C.U. Nov.1995.

phone or connected by internet. Long courtships should usually be avoided for the same reason."

To be drawn into LUSTS AND SINS will:

A. Destroy the esteem a Christian couple should have for each other.

B. Destroy much of the joy and pleasure that sex has in marriage—once something is abused it is hard to enjoy.

Should you ever date an unbeliever? The simple answer is NO! You should never marry one! (II Cor 6:14; Deut 7:2–3; Judg 3:6; Amos 3:3; and Ezra 9:1–2). The unbeliever's world and life view is opposed to God and he or she cannot exhibit *agape* love. Mixed marriages with unbelievers were the cause of global spiritual declension and ultimately the flood in Genesis 6:2–7 and the cause of much grief to the people of Israel, including Ezra, in Ezra chapters 9 and 10. But Paul leaves us in no doubt. Marriage is a one flesh union of body and spirit. A mixed couple cannot edify or sanctify one another. Look what happened to Samson and Solomon!

The unbeliever will inevitably bring down the believer and the statistics are against the ultimate conversion of the unbeliever. Intermarrying with the heathen always led Israel into idolatry. There are many couples where a believer has sinned in marrying an unbeliever in which the unbelieving spouse remains an unbeliever for many, many years into the marriage, causing much heartache. There is no guarantee they will ever be converted. Speak to anyone in a spiritually mixed marriage and hear their problems and think twice if you are tempted.

One major reason you should not date or marry an unbeliever is that they have no resources to truly love you. Only a relationship with God that satisfies, fulfils and brings joy, through the operation of the Holy Spirit, gives the freedom to reach out and to love another person rather than always manipulate, take and consume. An unbeliever is an idolater (of self) and so when he says, "I love you," he means, "You are a means for getting what I want. You are serving my needs and securing my hopes." For the Christian, manipulation is replaced by ministry as the couple serves one another loving God and their neighbor. You have to remember that personal fulfilment will not come even in the most wonderful romantic (and sexual) relationship. Only *God* can fill that spiritual need. Pascal rightly stated, "In every man there is a *God*-shaped vacuum."

The Samaritan woman at the well (John 4) looked in vain for supply of her deep needs through a succession of lovers but only Messiah Jesus could give her the eternal life-supplying water of the Spirit. Before you start courting anyone examine your motives:

- Is it to make me feel more secure?
- Is it just to escape loneliness?
- Is it to keep up with friends and peer pressure?

When courting is selfish or idealistic then God's word is placed under feelings. Sex and courting need to be under the Spirit's dominion. In courting, the man is to lead and bless—he is not to exploit the woman in any way. The enemy within is selfish, insensitive and uncommitted. Love God and your neighbor. Far too few think of courting as an opportunity to honor God, and this commitment requires us to put our courting partner's holiness ahead of our happiness. The foundations for a healthy and godly marriage begin while we are courting. According to the Bible's perspective, if you are dating you are not just holding hands, but holding *hearts*. Before you start courting, in the fellowship and group of young people in the church, you must find out what the general direction of her life is, namely, studies or job, Christian service, and so on. Remember: God has a specific unique person if it is his will that you marry. At this point I want to quote extensively from Rev. Van Overloop's booklet, *Sex and Dating in the Christian Life*.

Effects of Premarital Sex

> "At the outset, as blood-bought believers and followers of the Lord Jesus Christ, we must agree that the number one priority of our lives should be our relationship with Him and for this to flourish we are told in Psalm 24:3–5:

> "Who shall ascend into the hill of the LORD? or who shall stand in his holy place? He that hath clean hands, and a pure heart; who hath not lifted up his soul unto vanity, nor sworn deceitfully. He shall receive the blessing from the LORD, and righteousness from the God of his salvation."[6]

Then listen to Josh Harris,

> "Physical intimacy is much more than two bodies colliding. God designed our sexuality as a physical expression of the oneness of marriage. God guards it carefully and places many stipulations on it because He considers it extremely precious. A man and a woman who commit their lives to each other in marriage gain the right to express themselves sexually to each other. A husband and a wife may enjoy each other's bodies because they in essence belong to each other. But if you are not married to someone, you have no claim on that person's body, no right to sexual intimacy."[7]

There are many reasons why sex and sexual arousal should be kept for marriage. First, as your Creator, and also of all men and women and of sex, He knows best! A life of obedience honors God, blesses you and brings fruitfulness. Rev. Van Overloop writes,

> "It is helpful to consider what happens when we disobey God. If we misuse His good gift of sexuality, what are the consequences? "Be not deceived; God is not mocked: for whatsoever a man soweth, that shall he also reap" (Gal 6:7). "Flee sexual immorality" (I Cor 6:18). Sexual sin is against your body and the indwelling Spirit, it is defiling His temple! The girl who violates God's commands concerning sex feels used and cheated. She realizes, too late, that she has "lost" a most precious possession: her virginity. "Lost," however, is not really the right word, because she gave it away cheaply. Virginity is a gift God gave her. It is not really hers, but God's, and she is but the steward of it. She is responsible to God for its care. She

6. Van Overloop, Sex and Dating, p7.
7. Harris, Kissed Dating Goodbye, p94

can give her virginity away only once. She can never get it back. She will never be able to give this precious gift to her God-given husband at the proper time. Today's society says very little about the pricelessness of virginity. To the contrary, television, movies, and romance novels make virginity cheap. They sacrifice it on the altar of "fun." While I am convinced that most girls do prize it, they face many and great temptations to give it away. Some do not want to be considered "odd." Others want the feeling now.

Many think they can use sex to get love. Many give in to their boyfriend's pleas because they do not want to lose his "love." In every case, however, it is selfishness that has made them violate God's will. And the consequences are irreversible. The young man also "loses" something when he goes too far before marriage. He also gives away a priceless gift, and he does so cheaply. The loss of innocence, through sexual impurity, is as real for the boy as it is for the girl. He may deceive himself into believing that the gratification of the moment will make that loss worthwhile. But he too will find, to his great grief, that it does not. For God will not be mocked. All sexual activity before marriage is entering into a holy of holies in a degrading, base, and profane manner, violating the will of God. And the only reason for rushing so boldly into this holy and beautiful mystery is the selfishness of pride. I want, and I want it now! Some claim the "right" to premarital sex because they are engaged to be married. They believe that their expressions of commitment to each other make it right for them to violate God's will. But consider the reasons for wanting to go contrary to God's command! Every one of them is wrong: self-gratification, the desire to be loved, the fear of what the partner will think. Can such motives and such action be defended before an open Bible? It is God's will that sex be only in marriage. And it is only God who unites two in marriage, using the church and the state to be His means to unite them. A couple is not married merely on the basis of their commitment to each other. (Or if they live together, there has to be a public ceremony with or without vows, as exemplified in Malachi 2:14—JK). The command of our God is of course sufficient reason to refrain from premarital sex. There is however this added consideration, that not always do an engaged couple end up marrying each other. Should they break off their engagement, after engaging in sexual intercourse, they can be sure that, when they do marry, the pleasure of the marriage bed will not be unaffected by the memory of what went before. Sin may deceive us into thinking we can get away with it, but God is not mocked. Premarital sex always causes scars! Sin leaves scars. And the scars will have an effect on you years later. In the passion of the moment, you do not think about the implications and consequences which reach far beyond that moment. You do not want to think about the consequences. But this sin makes a searing cut, which always leaves a scar. Shame and pain will be your lot. You cannot violate the command of God concerning something so wonderful, and not be hurt by it. Sexual relationships many years later, with the husband and with the wife you love so dearly, are going to be affected by the illicit and immoral sexual activity which took place before you were married. I might add that many have been the counselling sessions with those whose improper sexual activity before marriage was with the one they did later marry. They judge each other, they blame each other, or they are plagued in conscience. When will we realize that God will not be mocked? We will reap what we sow! Sin leaves scars."[8]

More about this in an article that follows by Garrett Kell. For many, putting things right will mean breaking off sinful relationships!

> "There can be healing from the wound which sin causes, but there will always be a scar. This scar will be removed only when we receive our resurrection bodies. Please consider the scars you will cause, for yourself and for the one you love, before you rush into intimacy before God permits it."[9]

8. Van Overloop, Ibid, p6–7
9. Kell, Gospel Coalition, on-line.

There are other possible repercussions of sex outside marriage like an unwanted pregnancy and even venereal disease. If you have sinned,

> "He who created sexual desires and who redeemed them from being only powerful lusts of the flesh is also gracious in providing us a way of escape from the guilt and tyranny of lust. There is hope for those who have already violated God's pure gift of virginity. There is hope for those who desire to maintain the gift of purity which God gave them. There is hope for those who feel that the power of sex is out of control in their lives.

This comforting hope of divine healing is not for all. It is only for those with heartfelt sorrow and for those with an earnest desire to do God's will. First, God's healing is the power of His sovereign grace to remove the guilt of sin. Grace is the power which delivers from the filth of our sinful flesh. We may not be able to get our virginity back (even as we cannot remove a hole after pulling out the nail), but we receive God's gracious forgiveness. Immorality is not a sin which cannot be forgiven. Sexual sins and temptations are to be treated as all other sins and temptations—they are to be confessed, repented of, and forsaken. The prayer for God's forgiveness and for God's grace to walk in holiness must be lifted up to Him. Then there may be the assurance of His gracious forgiveness. And He forgives completely. (Remember . . . justification, the declaration that a believer is righteous with the righteousness of Christ, is perfect and permanent! All our sins, past, present and future were paid for on the cross—JK). When He forgives, the sin is gone forever, never again to be brought against the sinner. As ugly as the sin is, forgiveness is more beautiful, and grace makes us beautiful before God. We cannot retrieve our virginity, but we can retrieve our chastity and our purity before God. When God forgives, then He gives us a perfect righteousness. It is as if we had never sinned. It is as if we only did everything right. Therefore we hide ourselves under the wings of the righteousness and holiness which Jesus earned for us and which God imputes and imparts to us. Then we may be sure that we stand before God in pure, white robes, and we are called "Holy unto the Lord." Virginity is a precious gift, but an even more precious gift is forgiveness. Secondly, the Spirit of Christ brings, with complete forgiveness and perfect righteousness, the healing power of deliverance from sin's power along with the spiritual gift of self-control (called "temperance" in Galatians 5:23). Sexual energies and desires, no matter how strong, are controllable. As powerful as they may be, they can be controlled, for the power that is for us is greater than the power that is against us. The Bible teaches that we are not helpless before these lusts. It is Christ, to whom is given power over heaven and earth, who strengthens us (Phil 4:13). It is the divine Spirit whose fruit is self-control. We can therefore break with sinful self-indulgence. We are called not simply to maintain but also to develop Spirit-filled self-control. Jesus spoke of those who were eunuchs for the kingdom of heaven's sake (Matt 19:12). He spoke of self-control and self-denial for the sake of God's glory. And He declared that any man who would follow Him must practice self-denial (Matt 16:24), just like the Master, whose supreme self-denial brought about the salvation of sinners.

There are sins against which believers are commanded to stand and fight. But the only way the Bible says we are to fight sexual sin and temptation is to "flee" it (I Cor 6:18). Consider how Joseph fled from Potiphar's wife. This temptation is the kind that cannot be faced head-on. Will-power and resolutions do not stand a chance before this sin in particular. It is too strong. To think that we can be "brave" and stand up to this sin, is to be the fool. The only way to be faithful to God in regard to this sin is to flee it. The admonition to "flee fornication" has the clear implication that we must not over-estimate our self-control or our spirituality. That is why we are admonished to "make no provision for the flesh to fulfil the lusts thereof" (Rom. 13:14). To control sexual desires, we must realize the importance of avoiding situations where we know we will be tempted by the wiles of the devil. To control sexual desires one needs more wisdom than Solomon, for Solomon fell often to this temptation. One way not to make provision for the flesh to fulfil its lusts while courting is to "be alone with others, never all alone." Date along with others. Also stay away from every form of pornography—it is not "harmless." Another way to fight the temptation of this sin is by making a commitment, before we court, to be pure. This means that you must draw the line as to how far you will go. You need to draw a line before you court, because of how powerful the Bible tells us physical attraction is. We cannot have developing romantic love without having increasing desire for consummation. We are fools to deny this. It is abnormal to become more and more intimate mentally and emotionally and not want to become more and more intimate physically and sexually. You are playing with fire if you keep getting closer and closer together when you are not ready to marry. We need to draw the line before we date, because wavering at the beginning often results in our falling in the end."[10]

In an article entitled "Satan's Strategy To Destroy Your Marriage Before It Ever Begins," Garrett Kell, of Del Ray Baptist Church (Alexandria, Virginia) makes the following crucial points for consideration:

> "Many unmarried Christian couples struggle with sexual sin. And this should be no surprise, we have an enemy who is set against us and set against our impending marriage (1 Pet. 5:8). This enemy hates God and he hates marriage because it depicts the gospel (Eph. 5:32). One of Satan's most effective strategies to corrupt the gospel-portraying union of marriage is to attack couples through sexual sin before they say "I do." Here are four of his most common ploys to attack marriages before they begin.
>
> *1. Satan wants us to make a pattern of obeying our desires instead of God's direction.*
>
> God's ways are good, but Satan wants us to believe they aren't. This has been his plan from the first call to compromise in the garden (Gen 3:1–6). His end goal is for us to develop a consistent pattern of resisting the Spirit and following our sinful desires once we get into marriage. He wants us to learn to resist service and to pursue selfishness. If we learn to do what we want when

10. Van Overloop, Ibid. p8–9

we want before marriage, we'll carry that pattern into the days and years that follow. This, however, is deadly since service and sacrifice are essential to a healthy, Christ-honoring marriage. Love in marriage is shown by a thousand daily decisions to do what you don't want—whether doing the dishes or changing a diaper . . . If your relationship before marriage is characterized by giving into urges of immediate desire, you'll most certainly struggle when you encounter the nitty-gritty of married life.

2. *Satan wants us to underestimate how susceptible we are to temptation.* Satan wants us to think we won't take our sin to the next level. He wants us to think we're stronger than we really are. He wants us to think we'll never go that far. This is a powerful trick since it simultaneously plays on both our pride and also our well-intended desire to honor God. You're weaker than you think. You can go where you think you won't. Sin is like an undercurrent in the ocean—if you play in it, you'll be overpowered and swept away into certain destruction. One of the ways Satan works this angle is by tempting you to think purity is a not-to-be-crossed line rather than a posture of the heart. He wants you to think purity before God is not kissing or not taking off clothes . . . or not "going all the way." He wants you to think that if you don't cross a certain line, you're staying pure. The problem with this kind of thinking, however, is that Jesus says if we just lust in our heart we've sinned and stand condemned before God (Matt. 5:27–30). Purity is much more about the posture of our hearts than the position of our bodies. The age-old "How far is too far?" question may reveal a desire to get as close to sin as possible instead of a desire to flee as our Lord calls us to (1 Cor 6:18).

3. *Satan wants couples to weaken their trust for each other.*

When we compromise sexually, we're showing the other person we're willing to use and abuse them to get what makes us happy. Every time we push the boundaries with our fiancée or lead her into sin we are communicating, though we don't mean to, "You can't trust me because I'm willing to use and disregard you to get what

I want." This is certainly one of Satan's deadliest strategies . . . It's important to point out, however, that when we resist sexual sin, God blesses a relationship with the exact opposite effect. Every time we say "no" to sexual sin and turn to prayer, telling one another we value them and their walk with the Lord too much to go one step further, he uses that faithfulness to strengthen trust. My wife regularly tells dating couples that one of the reasons she trusts me is because I literally ran from compromising situations before we were married. We weren't perfect in our courtship, but the Lord used that season to build trust in one another.

4. Satan wants to deceive you with the forbidden fruit of lust.

There's a world of difference between premarital sex and sex within marriage. One reason is that the forbidden fruit of lust portrays sex before marriage as something it isn't always in marriage. Normally, premarital sexual activity is like gas on fire. Passion is high, feelings are intense, and the drive to go further is fueled by the knowledge you shouldn't (Rom 7:8). Sex in marriage is different. There's still passion, and there's still intense feelings and emotions—but sex in marriage is based primarily on the hot coals of trust, devotion, and sacrifice (1 Cor 7:1–5). Couples who built their sexual expectations on passion provided by the forbidden fruit are often disappointed and confused when sex is different in marriage. My wife and I laughed at this idea when our premarital counselor shared it with us. We were sure we'd be the exception to the rule. But almost six years and three kids later, he was right. Couples like us can have a strong sex life, but it's fueled by deeper characteristics than fleeting passion. Satan wants couples to get used to running on the caffeine and sugar of lust rather than mature love of service and sacrifice.

A Few Concluding Thoughts

1. Wait in faith. The Christian posture is always one of waiting. We wait for Christ's return. We wait for an eternity with him. And unmarried believers wait for the blessings of marriage. Say "no" to sin's promises by faith in God's. Renew your mind with God's Word and keep waiting in faith.

2. *Guys, you gotta lead.* While both persons in the relationship are responsible before God, the man must set the pace for purity. Too often ladies are forced to draw the lines and to say "no." That's cowardly and wrong. It's the man's responsibility to care for his future wife by leading her toward Jesus and away from sin, darkness, and the pain of evil. If he sets the wrong pattern here, he'll be digging out for years afterward—and may never regain the ground he loses apart from God's grace.

3. *Involve others every step of the way.* Don't let your relationship remain unexamined by other godly Christians. Both of you should have a godly couple or group of faithful friends who hold you accountable. Invite tough questions and give honest answers. God uses transparency to give strength.

4. *If you sin, go to the gospel.* The apostle John wrote, "My dear children, I write this to you so that you will not sin. But if anybody does sin, we have one who speaks to the Father in our defense—Jesus Christ, the Righteous One" (1 John 2:1–2). If you sin, flee to the cross. Run to the empty tomb. Look to your Advocate, confess your sin deeply, and repent. God loves to bless this kind of posture (Prov 28:13). Sexual sin doesn't need to be a dagger in the heart of your courting relationship, engagement, or marriage. God is a merciful God who delights in restoring what sin seeks to destroy (Joel 2:25–27). He will not, however, bless ongoing disobedience and presumption on his grace. If you have fallen into sexual sin, today is the day to plead for mercy and turn to Christ in faith. May God give us mercy to pursue purity for his glory and our good."[11]

11. Kell, Gospel Coalition website.

Motivations

Some motivations for not having sex before marriage are wrong. They can be just as wrong as having sex before marriage. One such wrong motivation is *fear*: fear of being found out, fear of pregnancy, fear of a disease, or fear of the opinions of others. One proper motivation for doing God's will is love of our neighbor. The neighbor we are to love as ourselves can be our neighbor's daughter. Also, your neighbor can be one who will be your wife. And your neighbor is your parents or your future wife's parents, both of whom would be hurt terribly when your sin is discovered.

But the main motivation is our love of God. Love God for the salvation He has so freely given. Love God for all things, including the sexual desires He has given. Submit your sexuality, along with everything else you are and have, to Him. Let your love for Him drive you to strive to please him in all of your conduct, including your conduct on a date.

Conclusion

I have no desire to give you a list of rules. Law only provokes to more sin (Rom 7:5, 8). Rather, I will leave you to the custody of the guidelines and thoughts of the Word of God as we have just written about them. You, in light of the Bible, must judge whether you are misusing God's wonderful gift of sexual desires. Do not forget that the woman or the man whom you lust after in your heart (called "adultery" in Matthew 5:28) may be the one you are dating! You can come to your wedding night without ever having kissed, and not lose one thing, like Harris and Shannon. Many have lost much who kissed on the first date and kept going from there!

Brandon Anderson, in an article entitled "Notes on Dating for Guys," writes the following:

> "The Bible only outlines two categories for Christian women in relation to Christian men: either she is a sister in Christ or she is your wife. There isn't a middle ground. The lie is, "We're halfway married, so we can do 50% of

the married things." That is not true at all. You need to put physical touch in two categories: acts of affection or acts of desire. Acts of affection are ways that you show that you like, appreciate, and cherish the women that you are dating. Think of it as a affectionate father with his daughter. He hugs her, snuggles her, kisses her on the forehead, holds her hand, stopping at any type of sexual satisfaction whatsoever. He just wants to make sure his daughter knows that he loves her. Acts of desire are acts that are reserved for marriage. Foreplay is designed for one purpose: to build the desire to have sex, which it does well. Think of foreplay like and freeway on-ramp: it's purpose is to transition you to full speed. You don't see cars hanging out on on-ramps, never intending to get on the freeway. Physical touch is designed to progress, and it is naive to think you will always be able to keep your desires in check. Failure and sin is all but inevitable. In short, you know what you are doing. If you stop for a moment and think about it, you know which category the physical touch you are doing falls into. It is different for everyone. It is not helpful for me to tell you where the line is so that your conscience will allow to you run up to that line and hang out there for a while (Titus 2:6). If you are asking the question "How far can we go and still be in the clear?" your heart is in the wrong place to begin with. I would encourage any couple who is focused on the physical to change their focus to friendship (Song of Sol 2:7). Building a friendship will set you up for a strong marriage far more than a physical connection. The physical connection will come later, you don't have to worry about that. But you have freedom, in the midst of gospel community, to pursue friendship and have fun."[12]

He's Called Us to Holiness

There is a right way, there is a best way, and they are both the same way: God's way (I Thess 4:3–8). God did not give us rules just to

12. Anderson, male2man.com

steal all of our fun; he's called us to holiness, and the rules are for our joy and protection. The process of courting is an exercise in putting Christ on the throne in all things. So embrace it, and don't just endure it. By the grace of God, hold fast to the teaching, the warnings, and the admonitions of God's Word. Strive to be pure as the Lord your God is pure. Purity or chastity is losing your life (your desires) for Jesus' sake, and having the promise of finding them (Matt 16:25). Be willing to lose your life (a life of sexual satisfaction before marriage) for the sake of Christ your Savior. God made your body, and in it He gave you the gift of virginity. And He gave you His Son to redeem you soul and body, both of which are not yours, but His (I Cor 6:19–20). The gift of your virginity can be given away only once. Keep it for your God-given mate. And believe God's promise of joy and fulfilment. Great will your reward be in heaven. "But put ye on the Lord Jesus Christ, and make not provision for the flesh, to fulfil the lusts thereof" (Rom 13:14).

Study Questions

1. What are some of the conditions or irreducible complexities that must be fulfilled before conception occurs?
2. When does a human being start? Prove this from Scripture.
3. What major influences are brought to bear on young people today in the sexual realm?
4. What are the essential elements of a satisfying friendship?
5. Describe the different kinds of love?
6. What is the basic difference between true love and a "crush"?
7. List some important questions that need to be answered in the affirmative about a prospective marriage partner?
8. List as many reasons as you can to abstain from sex till marriage?
9. What happens if you don't?

Chapter 16

The Wedding is Soon

It is interesting that the Bible begins and ends with a marriage and that the first miracle Jesus performed was at a wedding. So now you are engaged and you have told friends and relatives, perhaps put an advertisement in the paper or a page on "The Knot" website. It is important that you have been frank and open with your future spouse about past loves and mistakes (I John 1:7). Engagement is not a license for sex. There is a time to embrace, namely, after marriage, and a time to refrain from embracing (including any sort of petting), before marriage (Eccl 3:5). Disagreements are no indication you are not compatible. Learn to say "sorry"—a vital word in any relationship. How long should your engagement be? If you live near one another and see each other a lot then six months may be sufficient. My courtship was conducted mainly by letter and lasted a year, but we were engaged and married within a month!

Things to talk about before the wedding include mutual interests, church membership and service, where to live, standard of living, use of the home, food, money, children, birth-control, in-laws, the wedding itself and the honeymoon. Attend marriage preparation classes with your pastor or elder. Engagement should be a solemn covenant to marry. Joseph nearly divorced his fiancée Mary, when they were betrothed which in those days was like a marriage bond. God keeps His promises. So should we. Only proven unfaithfulness should be a reason for breaking an engagement or separation in marriage. Plan the wedding with the responsible parents and the pastor, and make it a testimony to God's covenant faithfulness, especially to any unsaved family members.

Chapter 17

Family Planning

THIS ISSUE IS CONTROVERSIAL and I shall attempt to give a balanced biblical and Reformed view.

The best preparation for sexual intercourse, by consenting married couples, the only people God sanctions with this activity, is consistent loving behavior throughout the day, with each serving the other. Generally, intercourse takes place in their bed, in private, with the door locked if they have children, tenants or visitors staying. It is a good idea to empty bladder and bowel before getting into bed. Foreplay is the prelude to intercourse in which the couple will caress, kiss and stimulate each other by touch which gets more and more intimate, leading to a moistening of the woman's vagina and an erection in the man. Lubricating jelly is often a necessary adjunct to help penetration. You need to discuss contraception before you get married. John 1:12 mentions birth by the will of man and it is true that God has given us the ability to will or not will the birth of a baby which is in contrast to spiritual regeneration which is His divine prerogative. Just as He has given us drugs to control pain He has given contraceptive methods for the benefit of man, when used correctly and morally. Jesus Himself advocated the use of a physician (Matt 9:12), so we must never shun medical help or the discoveries of modern medicine. It is a reasonable suggestion that a time of adjustment after getting married where husband and wife wait before starting a family is a good idea. The law allowed for a newlywed soldier to take a year at home before embarking on a military career with the Israelite army (Deut 24:5). This would also apply if the courtship was conducted at a distance, e.g., over the internet or by letter. Some would argue that we have as a race obeyed the command to be fruitful and multiply and the world population being what it is means it is necessary to limit the size of families. On the other hand, Psalm 127:5 says the man who has his quiver full of arrows (children) is happy. You must decide under God. In any case there are various methods to prevent conception, one very natural and various others. The Christian woman should never use the IUD (intrauterine device) or the progesterone-only pill because, rather than prevent conception they prevent implantation of the early embryo, thus they are an early cause of abortion. The IUD can also cause infection and heavy periods. The scriptural teaching is that life begins at conception and individuals are known from the womb and often regenerated before birth, soon after or in infancy (e.g., Jer 1:5; Ps 13; Luke 1). Psalm 139 outlines the amazing way God weaves together the tissues that make a human being in the embryo, during the first eight weeks, and later the fetus, before birth. The writer, who is the subject of the psalm was the sweet psalmist of Israel, namely, King David.

The "morning after" pill is also an early abortifacient, which means it causes the death of an early conception, by preventing implantation, and thus is unlawful for the believer. The oral contraceptive pill, or "the pill," is the most reliable method (with a 3 percent failure rate) comprising of hormones that prevent ovulation. However it appears that if ovulation does occur leading to conception, it also works by thinning the lining of the womb, thus acting as an early abortifacient and for this reason the conscientious believing couple should choose another method. The durex, condom, sheath, or French letter (all synonyms) is also very reliable and cheap. It is a simple thin rubber barrier that the male slips over his penis before intercourse. The couple may or may not use spermicide creams along with it. The "rhythm method" (or "safe period") in which a couple only have intercourse several days after ovulation (gauged by a rise in temperature) is natural but less reliable than the other methods. Ovulation is assumed when a) the mouth of the vagina feels wet, b) there is a sharp pain felt on one side of the lower abdomen, c) a pink spot appears on the underwear, d) the breasts tingle and e) the temperature taken on waking (rectal, oral or vaginal) is raised above normal. The period when a woman is most likely to conceive is the six days before the temperature rise and the first two days into the rise, that is, six days prior to and two days after ovulation. If day one is taken as the first day of the period or monthly cycle, then assuming the period lasts the first five days and you avoid intercourse during that period, then days 6 to 8 and days 17 to 28 are the safe period, but this is NOT fool-proof or very reliable! As far as I know this is the preferred method of devoted Roman Catholics. Sterilization is the ultimate method of contraception where usually one partner agrees to undergo minor surgery when either the male undergoes a vasectomy under local anesthesia (both tubes cut) or the female has her fallopian tubes cut and tied off or clipped laparoscopically (through an incision in the abdomen, under general anesthetic using a thin telescopic instrument called a laparoscope. These methods can be reversed but ought to be entered into with irreversibility in mind. I am now going to quote from one of several articles on the theme "Moral Aspects of Medical Technology" by Prof. Herman C. Hanko.

> "By contraception I refer to whatever means are used to prevent the conception of a child. This may range from various types of materials used to prevent conception, through sterilization procedures, to what is usually called the rhythm method. There are three points which need to be made at the outset. The Scriptures give us no warrant to condemn the use of contraceptives or contraceptive procedures out of hand. This is evident from two considerations: 1) Various contraceptives, such as "the pill," can be used for medicinal purposes to correct various malfunctions of the body, even though they, at the same time, make conception (almost—JK) impossible.

2) There are circumstances when parents have no choice but to make use of contraceptives, especially when the life of the mother is threatened by pregnancy, e.g., severe heart disease. The second point that needs to be made is that God's people are called upon to live consciously and responsibly before God in every area of their life, including marriage and bringing forth children. People are not to breed as animals, by instinct; they are to use marriage and sex within marriage as gifts of God to His glory, consciously seeking the honor of God's name also in this important part of their life. The third point is that intercourse itself is a gift of God to be used by husbands and wives within the marriage state as an expression of their love for each other. It can be, and is, an expression of love entirely apart from the conception of children. This is clear from the fact that to hold to a different position would simply mean that husbands and wives who are unable to have children or who are beyond the age of child-bearing would then not have the right to engage in intercourse. All of this means that contraception belongs to the realm of Christian liberty and the rightness or wrongness of it must be judged on the basis of the motives in the hearts of those who make use of these methods.

We all know that liberty can easily become licentiousness. Paul speaks of this in Galatians 5:13: "For, brethren, ye have been called unto liberty; only use not liberty for an occasion to the flesh, but by love serve one another." Liberty becomes an occasion to the flesh when young people outside the marriage state, engage in fornication, but use contraceptive methods to avoid the consequences of pregnancy. This is an abomination to the Lord, and no fornicator can enter the kingdom. Liberty becomes an occasion for the flesh when married people engage in adultery and use contraceptive methods to prevent pregnancy. This too is an abomination to God and will surely bring upon the sinner God's just wrath. But even within the marriage state the use of contraceptive methods can be and is judged by God to be wrong and sinful when their use is for the wrong motives. Those motives may be many and we mention only a few of them. It is part of the "climate" of our sophisticated age not to have large families. I myself well recall how shocked some people were when I or my wife told them we had eight children. Besides, children are a bother and a nuisance. It is not fun to have howling babies in the house, to have to get up in the middle of the night to feed them, to mop up their vomit when they are sick, to put up with their incessant demands, to rinse out their dirty diapers, etc. There are people who do not want to have children because the "strain" of bringing them up is too great. There are people who do not want children because they are too expensive to feed, clothe, educate, and prepare for life. (Have you heard of "DINKS"? Double income no kids!—JK) There are parents who do not want to have children because children keep them from vacations, parties, skiing holidays, bowling, and all kinds of pleasure which their souls crave. There are parents who do not want children, at least not very many, because the mother wants to work. The parents like the extra income because it enables them to buy the good things of life. All these motives are sinful and God hates them. To use contraceptives for such purposes is evil and brings God's disapproval. The Bible takes quite a different view of life than this. The purpose of marriage is to bring forth children; specifically, the purpose of a covenant marriage is to bring forth covenant children (Mal. 2:14ff). While God does not always make that possible because some parents are prevented from having children, nevertheless, the institution of marriage is for that very reason. When God joined Adam and Eve in marriage, He added this word to the institution: "Be fruitful, and multiply, and replenish the earth."Covenant parents bring forth covenant children. Covenant parents are deeply impressed with their calling and obligation, not only to bring up their children in the fear of the Lord, but to bring forth children, for God has given them the great privilege of bringing forth the church of our Lord Jesus Christ. In a wonderful and mysterious way, God uses covenant parents to bring forth that number of elect whom He has chosen from all eternity, whom He has given to Christ, who are redeemed through the blood of the cross, and who are destined to live in covenant fellowship with God through Christ in the new heavens and the new earth. God will, of course, see to it that His church is born. He has His own elect number, engraved on the palms of His hands. Not one shall fail to be born, to be saved and to be brought to heaven. Covenant parents, conscious of this and conscious of the privilege of bringing forth this church, understand that marriage is the institution which God has provided for this church to be brought forth. Godly parents, therefore, consider children to be a great blessing. How different this is in the world, where children are a curse and a bother. Children are a heritage of the Lord, and blessed is he whose quiver is full of them. In the covenant family, children are like olive plants round about our tables and the parents who are blessed see their children's children and peace upon Israel. So true is this that in the Old Testament we have many instances of godly women who saw their barrenness as a curse and who prayed earnestly for children. They did this in the consciousness that in having children they would have a part in bringing forth the Christ, who would be their Savior. This has not changed in the New Testament. A woman is still saved through childbearing. None of us can be saved unless all of God's people are saved. The whole body of the elect goes to heaven, or none goes. Christ will not return until the last elect is born and brought to repentance, as Peter teaches in II Peter 3:9. In eagerness for the return of Christ and the full salvation of heaven, God's people bring forth children. And they do so, greatly in awe that God has given them such a wonderful privilege. In the light of all this must contraceptive methods be considered and used. It is, you see, a matter of the motive; but God knows the heart and judges every man according as he does things out of a true faith, in keeping with the law of God, and to God's glory. There are times when contraception is necessary. When parents, in deciding when to have a child or another child, want to wait a bit for good and spiritual reasons, abstinence (rhythm method) is the honorable way. You will say that this does not always work and is by no means "safe." That is true. But the believer stands in the consciousness of the fact that God gives us our children, and that ultimately each child fashioned in the womb is a work of God delicately and carefully done according to God's own counsel and will. (Every conception is a miracle of irreducible complexity—JK). There are times when other methods must be used. When the believer faces these times, he does so prayerfully and carefully, asking always, "Lord, what wilt thou have me do?" He is clearly concerned about the approval of God. Husbands and wives know that God's blessing on their marriage is indispensable and they live in the great fear that they will find themselves displeasing to God in this important and blessed part of their life. But they know that when they decide that God has so arranged the circumstances of their life that they must put off having children or refrain altogether, God will bless their decision. (A couple of examples would be the woman with a serious heart condition who might die in pregnancy and another would be woman in her fifties who is still fertile and, with her husband, believes they have completed their family and feel it would be wrong to have another child recognizing that fetal abnormalities greatly increase in frequency in pregnant women over forty and that they may die before the child is grown—JK). Pharaoh attempted to impose his own control over births upon the Israelites while they were in Egypt when he commanded all the baby boys to be drowned in the river. Israel refused to obey the king in this respect and did all they could to continue to have children and to hide them from the king when the children were born. The midwives cooperated in this. And God blessed them. The bringing forth of children was more important than the king's command.

It does indeed cost a lot of money to have children, bring them up, and educate them in the fear of the Lord. But we easily put a higher priority on earthly possessions than we do on children; and then we sin. Paul urges upon the church: "But godliness with contentment is great gain. For we brought nothing into this world, and it is certain we can carry nothing out. And having food and raiment let us be therewith content" (I Tim. 6:6–8).

The Lord has promised us that He will provide for all our needs. His promise has never failed. If we are content with our needs, we will be satisfied when the costs of children keep us from possessing the good things in life. We will find greater delight in our children than in houses and lands. We will know that we labor for eternity when we take care of our children, instead of laboring for things which pass away with the using. And when we and our children are finally safe in glory we will praise and honor Him who has given them to us."[1]

Study Questions

1. What is the purpose of courtship?
2. Why set standards for courtship?
3. Why is premarital sex, particularly for believers, so destructive?
4. What should you look for in a prospective wife or Husband?
5. List some issues that dating or engaged couples should discuss.
6. What methods of birth control should be avoided by the Christian?
7. Is birth control sinful?
8. If you are not a Reformed believer, how would you define the essentials of the Reformed Faith? Have you seriously considered your obligation to adopt them as your own?

1. Hanko, Moral Aspects of Medical Technology.

Appendix

The Reformed Faith

The Five Solas

THIS MEANS THAT WE maintain the biblical and apostolic gospel recovered in the sixteenth-century Protestant Reformation which is summarized in five famous "alones." The sixty-six books of the Bible are inspired ***Scripture alone*** and are the Word of God, the only infallible guide for faith and life (II Tim 3:16–17). The Bible reveals that all our salvation is in ***Christ alone***, as the only redeemer, mediator and head of the church (I Tim 2:5). The Lord Jesus delivers His people from the guilt, power and pollution of sin by ***Grace alone***, without our having to work for it (Eph 2:8–9). Salvation is received, known and enjoyed by ***Faith alone***, only by believing in Christ crucified and risen according to the gospel (John 6:47). The truths of Scripture alone, Christ alone, grace alone and faith alone serve the ***Glory of God alone***. This is what the church must proclaim and promote: the honor and glory of the Triune God revealed in Jesus Christ (Is 43:21)!

The T.U.L.I.P. abbreviation summarizes the points of Calvinism (explanation below)

Total depravity.

Unconditional election.

Limited atonement.

Irresistible grace.

Preservation of the saints.

We stand with that branch of the Reformation particularly associated with John Calvin and the doctrines of God's sovereign grace. We believe that fallen man is **totally depraved and completely unable to deliver himself**—or even contribute to his deliverance—from the bondage and misery of sin (Rom. 3:9–20).

But, before the foundation of the world, God, in His great mercy, **chose some** to salvation in Jesus Christ (Eph. 1:4). In the fullness of time, the Lord **Jesus laid down His life on the cross for his elect**, suffering for all of the sins of all of his sheep (John 10:11, 15). In due time, through the hearing of the gospel, **God grants a new spiritual heart to each of His elect** so that they all trust in his son alone (John 1:12–13). **Every true elect believer, being kept by the power of the Holy Spirit, perseveres in faith and holiness**, and will enter the joy of the Lord in the world to come either at death or the second coming of Christ (I Pet 1:3–5).

The Three Forms of Unity

These are statements of faith from the sixteenth and seventeenth centuries which Reformed churches believe are an accurate summary of Biblical doctrine and how it ought to be applied.

The Heidleberg Catechism

The Belgic Confession

The Canons of Dordt.

See my church website www.cprf.co.uk under 'Faith'.

Thanks for taking time to read this. I hope that you have profited from reading this booklet. You can write to me if you have any questions, criticisms or improvements and I shall try to answer but if you have not already, seek the faithful preaching of the word on Sundays in a true Reformed church.

Marks of a true church. http://www.cprf.co.uk/pamphlets/markstruechurch.htm#.UxjziD9FAic

Appendix

About the Author

Wedding Day October 25th 1985

Recent family snap

julikenn@doctors.org.uk

Bibliography

Alcorn, Randy. Eternal Perspective Ministries: http://www.epm.org/resources/1998/Sep/28/green-bay-packer-chapel-deuteronomy-17/

Anderson, Brandon. "Notes on Dating": http://male2man.com/2012/09/20/5-notes-on-dating-by-brandon-anderson/

Bartolomei, Tracey. "Courtship, Dating and Right Relationships" http://www.leaderu.com/common/courtship.html

Engelsma, David J. *Better to Marry*. Reformed Free Publishing Association, Grandville, MI: 1998.

———. Holiness in Marriage and Single Life. Protestant Reformed Theological Journal, Vol XXV No 1, Nov 1991.

———. *Marriage: The Mystery of Christ and the Church*. Reformed Free Publishing Association, Grandville, MI: 1998.

Hanko, Herman C. "Moral Aspects of Medical Technology," the *Standard Bearer*, vol 62, issue 18 (7/1/1986).

Hanko, Ronald. "Study Outline for the Christian Union Departmental Group" (Religion and Philosophy Department), at Queen's University Belfast, 20 November 1995.

Harris, Joshua. *Boy meets Girl: Say Hello to Courtship*. Multnomah Books, Colorado Springs: 2000, 2005.

———.*I Kissed Dating Goodbye*. Multnomah Books, Colorado Springs: 1997.

Heidelberg Catechism (on-line): http://www.prca.org/about/official-standards/creeds/three-forms-of-unity/heidelberg-catechism

Kell, Garrett. "The Gospel Coalition" http://garrettkell.com/satans-strategy-to-destroy-your-marriage-before-it-begins/

Kleyn, Rodney. "The E-World and Our Teenagers," in the *Standard Bearer*, RFPA, vol. 82, issue 7 (1/1/2006).

Phillips, Richard and Sharon. *Holding Hands, Holding Hearts*. P&R, 2006.

Protestant Reformed Theological Journal, vol. 25, no. 1.

Quoist Michel, Prayers of Life, 1963.

Stewart, Angus. "The Importance of Creeds for Christian Youth": http://www.cprf.co.uk/articles/creedsforyouth.html#.UzHEpz9F2M8

Van Overloop, Ronald. *Sex and Dating in the Christian Life*. Southeast Protestant Reformed Church, Grand Rapids, MI: 1994. (http://www.cprf.co.uk/pamphlets/sexdatingchristianlife.htm).

Index of Scriptures

Index of Scriptures

Index of Scriptures

www.ingramcontent.com/pod-product-compliance
Lightning Source LLC
Chambersburg PA
CBHW070508090426
42735CB00012B/2691
* 9 7 8 1 5 3 2 6 1 6 4 3 3 *